A New Hearing

W9-BWV-393

A New Hearing

LIVING OPTIONS
IN HOMILETIC
METHOD

Richard L. Eslinger

ABINGDON
PRESS
NASHVILLE

A NEW HEARING: LIVING OPTIONS IN HOMILETIC METHOD(t)

Copyright © 1987 by Abingdon Press

96 97 98 99 00 01 02—10 9 8 7

All rights reserved.
No part of this work may be reproduced or transmitted in any form or by any
means, electronic or mechanical, including photocopying and recording, or
by any information storage or retrieval system, except as may be expressly
permitted by the 1976 Copyright Act or in writing from the publisher.
Requests for permission should be addressed to Abingdon Press,
201 8th Avenue South, P. O. Box 801, Nashville, TN 37202.

This book is printed on recycled acid-free paper.

Library of Congress Cataloging in Publication Data

Eslinger, Richard L. (Richard Lawrence), 1940-
A new hearing.
Includes bibliographies.
1. Preaching. 2. Sermons, American. I. Title.
BV4211.2E85   1987   251   86-22166

ISBN 0-687-27693-4 (pbk.: alk. paper)

Scripture quotations noted RSV are from the Revised Standard Version of the Bible,
copyrighted 1946, 1952, © 1971, 1973 by the Division of Christian Education of the
National Council of the Churches of Christ in the U.S.A., and are used by permission.

Scripture quotations noted TEV are from the Good News Bible, the Bible in Today's
English Version, copyright © American Bible Society, 1976.

From *As One Without Authority* by Fred Craddock. Copyright © 1979 by Abingdon Press.
Used by permission.
From *Preaching* by Fred Craddock. Copyright © 1985 by Abingdon Press. Used by
permission.
T. S. Eliot, "Choruses from 'The Rock' " from *Collected Poems, 1909-1962;* by permission
of Harcourt Brace Jovanovich and Faber and Faber Ltd.
From *Doing Time in the Pulpit* by Eugene Lowry. Copyright © 1985 by Abingdon Press.
Used by permission.
The Homiletical Plot: The Sermon As Narrative Art Form by Eugene L. Lowry, Copyright
1980 John Knox Press. Used by permission.
Quotations from *Black Preaching* by Henry Mitchell, copyright © by Henry Mitchell,
used by permission of author.
Quotations from "Interpretation and Preaching" by David Buttrick, in *Interpretation* 25,
no. 1 (January 1981), used by permission of *Interpretation.*

"Abraham and Isaac" by David Buttrick, from *Pulpit Digest* (January/February 1986).
Copyright © by Pulpit Digest Incorporated 1986. Used by permission.
"Just Look at Us Now" by Deneise Deter-Rankin reprinted by permission of author.
"The Providence of God" by Henry Mitchell reprinted by permission of author.
"A Sermon for Pentecost Day" by Charles Rice reprinted by permission of author.
"Swept Upstream" by Eugene Lowry reprinted by permission of author.
"Surrounded," copyright © 1979 by Fred B. Craddock, reprinted by permission of
author.
"The Wilderness and the Dry Land" from John Vannorsdall, "Esthetics and
Preaching," *dialog* 20, no. 2 (Spring 1981). Used by permission of *dialog.*

MANUFACTURED IN THE UNITED STATES OF AMERICA

To my students at
Duke University Divinity
School

Preface

The writing of *A New Hearing* has a place within the story of my own homiletical formation, or more precisely, lack of formation. This is not to say that I did not have an adequate grounding in the time-honored orthodoxy of topical preaching. Through both the preaching that I experienced in my home church and that which I encountered in seminary, an understanding of what constituted preaching was clearly conveyed. Main ideas, clear outlining, and effective illustration were the ideals; my challenge as a novice was to "get with the program." And apparently I absorbed these skills well enough to satisfy both seminary professors and ecclesiastical superiors.

Armed with this well-tried homiletic, I began my pastoral ministry just as the 1960s were reaching their social and political crescendo. All of a sudden, preaching was attacked for its lack of "relevance," and many seminaries simply dismantled their homiletics departments or even entire degree programs. A few brave (or stubborn) schools soldiered on with an approach to preaching which was increasingly dissonant with the exciting "modern times." Those of us serving in pulpits week in and week out tried, for the most part, to forge some sort of accommodation between the old homiletic and the new times. Sermon organization loosened up a bit, topics shifted to "relevant" themes, and all sorts of dreadful jargon began to claim our rhetoric.

The next decade saw the emergence of vigorous new approaches to biblical interpretation, which simply did not fit the old homiletic. No longer was the object to find the message in the text; rather, the text was now being viewed as a distinctive world, with its own unique shape and theological intention. And there was talk of preaching as storytelling and of inductive rather than deductive methods. A confusing array of novel approaches to preaching were being promulgated, alongside the old standbys.

I suspect that my response to all this was typical of that of many pastors. My sermons became piecemeal concoctions, and I simply overlooked the theological implications of this crazy-quilt methodology. Other, more pressing, agendas were now on center stage (the liturgical renewal of the churches, in my case), and this "makeshift" homiletic would just have to do! However, it was not doing very well, either within the reformed liturgical context, within the new biblical studies, or within the radically altered hearing of the community of faith. Eventually, the strain of having to use this jury-rigged model to preach a sermon every week, plus being recruited to serve with the national worship office of The United Methodist Church, forced me to become familiar with contemporary approaches to biblical preaching. This book is the result of my venture in surveying the relatively uncharted terrain of the new homiletics. Its writing has been for me a time of homiletical reformation. My hope is that *A New Hearing* will make a contribution to your ministry of preaching as well.

Many persons have contributed to the writing of this book, most notably the homileticians whose work is surveyed here. For their gracious cooperation and willingness to provide sermons which model their approaches, I am deeply indebted. I am also grateful to Professor Richard Lischer, my colleague and friend at Duke University Divinity School, for his encouragement and support. My wife Elise has contributed greatly to the book through her own theological reflections and responses as well as through the gifts of her Mississippi literary sensibilities. Two wonderful persons at the Divinity School, secretaries Frances Parrish and Gail Chappell, wrought a manuscript out of indecipherable jottings. For these and for all who would have the gospel receive a new hearing, I am thankful.

TRINITY SUNDAY, 1986

Contents

Introduction

Preaching is in crisis. This awareness has been with us for some time now, reducing pastoral morale and congregational fervor. But the way out, toward new effectiveness in preaching, is not yet clear. What is quite evident, though, is that the old topical/conceptual approach to preaching is critically, if not terminally ill. No longer buttressed by scriptural interpretation or the cultural ethos, this old orthodoxy of a discursive homiletic method persists in many pulpits simply for lack of a clear-cut alternative. Preachers gather together in workshops on their craft and chuckle when the leader refers to "three points and a poem." Yet many pastors return from such events and continue to preach the propositions and illustrations mainly because for them "it's always been done this way," and it has become a familiar and seemingly harmless habit. The inertia is aided and abetted in some situations by the persistence of a preaching service in which Scripture is minimally in evidence and is separated from preaching by all sorts of other liturgical "preliminaries." As the great, last act of the preaching service, the sermon is not embarrassed either by proximity to the Word or by ritual acts of response which would imply that there has been some call. But for whatever reason, the old homiletic persists well past its prime and on into its decline.

It is not as if preachers are oblivious to the crisis, though. The blank stares and congregational inattention can be sensed by pastors who preach week in and week out. For most of us, the realization has long since occurred that the old conceptual preaching simply is not heard by most of those in attendance. It has ceased to be a "Word-event"; the words go out from the pulpit, but never even find their way into the consciousness of the hearers. Some of the stories may stick in the mind of the congregation, particularly the first-person kind, and maybe an idea or two gets hammered in. But what has been retained does not connect together, and even the remembered illustrations rarely "illustrate" the unremembered conceptual material. We know these things, recognize the symptomology, and feel the impotence of it all—and we look for a new way, a new way which will grant a new hearing to God's Word.

Those ministers who are seeking a new approach to biblical preaching, however, will not find one clear-cut methodological alternative. Instead, they will be greeted by a bewildering field of homiletical contenders. There is talk of inductive approaches, and storytelling, life-situational, and various liberation models, though there seem to be as many books written out of the old orthodoxy as there are books exploring some new perspective. Any church publisher's series on preaching will reflect this wild diversity of the recognizable old and the unfamiliar new in preaching. Sermon commentaries provide the same situation, with unpredictable swings in homiletic method occurring as each new commentator tries his or her hand at biblical interpretation and sermonic approach. Congregations, too, experience these methodological and stylistic shifts in slow motion, as preachers come and go. "Points" give way to stories which are displaced by subjective pulpit musings with perhaps further recurrences of "points" or outbreaks of stories. This confusion, in fact, may be occasioned not only by ministerial changes, but by ministerial experimentation as well. We are not sure where we are, and while some of us have taken to this kind of exploration, most of us have tinkered only a bit with the old method. The numbering of the "points" may be jettisoned, the outline loosened up a bit, and more stories are used now. But the crisis continues, and the new directions seem unclear.

In order to deal effectively with this crisis, two kinds of insight would seem to be needed by those who preach. On the one hand, there is a need for some quite precise analysis as to the nature of the pathology afflicting the old homiletic. We would like to have specific reasons for rejecting an approach to preaching that many of us worked laboriously to learn in seminary! On the other, clarity is needed in the midst of all the new approaches to the ministry of preaching. The field needs to be mapped, the terrain surveyed, before we can engage either in experiments with new approaches or in evaluations of them. So, the twin homiletical questions at the present time in the life of the church are, What is really the problem with the old conceptual method? and, Where do we go from here?

This mapping of the confusing terrain of homiletics today was greatly assisted when Wellford Hobbie noted that there seemed to be three major homiletical approaches which have moved significantly beyond the old topical preaching orthodoxy.[1] He saw emerging on the horizon first an inductive approach to preaching, then the narrative or story form, and finally a method based on the movement and structure of the biblical text. In all these new approaches, there is a keen attentiveness to sermonic form out of a new respect for the variety of shapes Scripture takes and out of a concern that the form of the sermon will capture the interest and attention of the congregation. "Our challenge," Hobbie observes, "is how to get the truth, the gospel, heard among the varieties of listeners before us."[2] Based on this initial mapping of the new homiletics, the present volume proposes to explore in some detail these three major movements as represented in the specific methods of five contemporary homileticians. Charles Rice will be examined with reference to his homiletics of storytelling, which he shares to a great extent with his mentor, Edmund Steimle. The black narrative tradition in preaching will be examined through the interpretative services of Henry Mitchell. An inductive approach to preaching will be developed through considering the writing of that movement's primary advocate, Fred Craddock. The interesting work of Eugene Lowry will be explored as a sort of bridge between the narrative and inductive forms. The homiletic method of David Buttrick represents the third alternative, which seeks to find the indicators for sermonic shape within the structure, movement, and intention of the biblical pericope. Finally, a postscript to our survey of homiletic methods will explore uncharted, but revealing intersections between hermeneutics and homiletic method. Also, the preaching of Deneise Deter-Rankin and John Vannorsdall will be analyzed with reference to a further possible homiletic method.

The intent of this volume on homiletic method will be to allow, as much as possible, each homiletician to have a new hearing. I consider all these colleagues to be offering living options in homiletic method, and the primary purpose here is accuracy in reporting and clarity in explication. The method within this book on method is first to explicate the respective homiletician's critique of the liabilities pertaining to the old homiletic. Then, the development of their work typically will involve considerations of biblical interpretation, hermeneutics, and the present situation in church and culture. Finally, the specific method presented by each of these advocates of a new homiletic will be developed in some detail followed by a section of evaluation. However, a crucial aspect of this uncovering of each approach is the addition of a sermon that was both written and preached by each of our homileticians.[3] The methods surveyed are aptly modeled by the respective sermons, and each sermon stands as both an example of that preacher's approach and as a test case of that homiletic method.

The crisis in preaching will ease, to be replaced by a renewed pulpit in the churches, when proclamation again involves a hearing of God's Word. Each of the homileticians whose work we are surveying would agree with Paul that "faith comes from hearing" (Rom. 10:17 TEV). In a time when the old forms are no longer heard, the development of new expressions of homiletical form and method is an urgent agenda of reform. And the time is now full for those of us who preach to grant these expressions of a new homiletic a new hearing, for ourselves, for the people to whom we preach, and for the sake of the gospel of Jesus Christ.

NOTES

1. F. Wellford Hobbie, "The Play Is the Thing: New Forms for the Sermon," *Journal for Preachers* 5, no. 4 (1982), pp. 17-23.

2. Ibid., p. 17.

3. Each of the homileticians surveyed in this volume would caution that the essential orality of the rhetoric of preaching works against putting sermons into print. Conversely, a highly polished literary sermon is much less effective as a vehicle of oral communication.

1

CHARLES RICE

Preaching as Story

"Let us consider the storyteller," Charles Rice suggests.[1] The way towards renewal of preaching is to be found in the recovery of storytelling. But before this venture can be undertaken, a consideration of preaching's recent history is necessary to clearly identify the issues related to this renewal. Whatever else, the recent homiletical tradition has been marked by a scarcity of story and of storytellers.

Rice is fond of telling the story of Duke University emeritus professor W. D. Davies, who, when asked his opinion of the revival of interest in preaching, described sermons as "just church bells." The sermon is "an easily recognized sound which is comforting for its familiarity and will be tolerated so long as it does not disturb early-morning sleep or some other important activity."[2] The image suggests an expectation that preaching will be dull and lifeless, though vaguely religious in its perceived message.

Moreover, preaching has become highly stereotyped in its cultural expressions and typically manifests a predictable dualism. There are sermons that comfort, disperse community morals, and in general reflect the status quo. On the other hand, there are sermons in which the preacher fulfills the role of the issue-oriented disquieter within a controlled frame of reference. The preacher, then, adopts most often the alternative roles of "moral arbiter" of a community's

Charles Rice is professor of homiletics, Drew University Theological School, Madison, New Jersey.

values, "the scrupulous social puppet," or the community's "alter ego" functioning to disquiet within predictable parameters.[3] In both cases, however, the pulpit is the captive of a deadening intellectualism. Preaching is an impersonal affair, utilizing a discursive style and language which keeps the preacher from disclosing his or her humanity. The dominating image of the preacher is that of an academic ideal and the language of preaching is that of the seminary classroom and the theological lecture hall.[4]

A second form of dualism is observed by Rice when preachers reach for subjectivity in the midst of this intellectualistic enterprise. Too often, this "personal" content becomes cheaply emotional, especially when the predictable illustration is employed to "humanize" the otherwise impersonal sermon.

> The discursive style evades human experience, and superficial emotionalism parodies the human situation. The delivery is likely to be stereotyped, which is another evasion. The preacher is apt to rely on canned illustrations; slices of human life are seen as lines for a performance rather than as the very locus of the incarnation—as if the purpose of living were to make sermons! And the result is pat, glib, and dead (*PTS,* p. 32).

That deadness, moreover, can be seen across an incredible span of culture and ideology. Liberalism, of course, is most clearly beholden to this positivist and propositional approach to the faith, but Rice also correctly observes that this impersonalism has its fundamentalist expressions as well. In both of these children of the Enlightenment, preaching embodies a kind of methodological schizophrenia. The dominant mode of communication is rationalistic discourse, which appeals to only a narrow segment within the range of human personality. On the other hand, when liberalism and fundamentalism typically seek a more affective response, the result is likewise divorced from life by virtue of its dependence on emotionalism. "Both make for homiletical docetism: the Word does not become flesh" (*JCB,* p. 22). The sclerotic state of the traditional pulpit relates not only to this predictable dualism of rationalism and emotionalism, however. There is a controlled frame of reference for the styles of preaching as well as for its content. Rice observes that the preacher, "in what he or she says, and in the *way* in which it is said, is closely identified in the minds of many church goers with the way it was or the way it ought to be" (*RPC*, p. 19). Given this pressure for the sermon to invoke nostalgia and/or a pietistic utopia, the style of preaching becomes as controlled as the content. Even subtle shifts in such stylistic considerations as tone, manner, length, and vocabulary can disturb these "deeply ingrained stereotypes and rigid expectations [which] surround the pulpit" (*RPC*, p. 19).

If the Word is to become flesh in the event of preaching, a new approach to Scripture is necessary. Preaching must become more biblical, but not in the sense of proliferating Bible quotes, or intensifying the use of proof texts. Such a misuse of Scripture only worsens the reductionist interpretation already seen in both liberalism and fundamentalism. God's Word is alienated from real human experience and is treated homiletically "much as one would give footnotes to a term paper" (*JCB*, p. 22). These forms of preaching have treated Scripture mostly as a sourcebook for illustrations and as a collection of religious ideas or propositions. What results from this obliteration of the earthly and colorful accounts within Scripture is a Bible which has become "a kind of textbook or a collection of briefs to be *used* by the preacher in making a didactic sermon" (*RPC*, p. 20). Biblical preaching is impossible to derive from such a canon.

Authentic biblical preaching, for Rice, begins in seeing that real humanity is expressed throughout Scripture. The Bible "is about real people, written by real men and women to persons trying to live on the earth together" (*JCB*, p. 25). There is an exciting vividness which radiates from the very earthy lives of these human beings. This new approach to the Bible listens for God's Word in the accounts of the biblical people; the Story of God's self-disclosure is presented in specific stories about concrete human experience. Since

Scripture is the witness to the stories *which express the Story,* the importance of storytelling in the interpretation of the Bible is decisive. With Amos Wilder, Charles Rice identifies the story as "a natural speech-form for the gospel."[5] For both the Old and New Testaments, revelation is conveyed through the literary medium of story. Story expresses the Christian tradition so decisively that it becomes the normative mode of biblical revelation. Storytelling, Rice affirms, "has a close affinity to both the content and form of Christian revelation" (*PS,* p. 190). It is, therefore, the hermeneutical key to interpreting Scripture; "the openness and ability to hear a story, to really enter in and follow a story, is essential to understanding the Bible" (*JCB,* p. 25). The identity of the Christian and of the Christian community is grounded in a tradition which, at its core, is composed of stories. This Story, then, in return interprets us and our stories. Such events as the Exodus, the Exile, and the Incarnation are at the heart of the story of salvation. Our identity and self-understanding derive from them. They are our story. And most decisively, "We have to *enter* the scriptures before we can hope to lead anyone else into a meeting with the tradition" (*RPC,* p. 25).

The hermeneutical significance of story is not restricted to an understanding of the Bible, for Rice. Story is essential as a means of exegeting our own experience as well. Our lives are best understood as narratives, and story best provides access to understanding our experience. "We need to learn to hear and tell our own stories—not just our individual experience, but the stories we share with a given community and humankind—as much as we need to enter in and follow the Bible's unfolding story of God's ways with us" (*JCB,* p. 25). The recovery of authentic preaching will emerge out of this encounter between the story-laden tradition and the stories of our common life. Biblical preaching involves the Story of Scripture and stories of our lives. Authentic humanity is possible when storytelling interprets the Bible and our own experience.

When preaching becomes biblical preaching, Charles Rice believes that the style of the sermon most significantly marks the shift. More than almost any other quality, it is one's homiletical style which best signals the state of one's preaching. Unrenewed preaching will show a "projective-discursive style"—in which the preacher is distanced from the real world of the tradition and contemporary life. There is a projection of personality from the pulpit while the preacher remains impersonal. Rice attacks this "personality without personhood" repeatedly.[6] Nothing can be further removed from the preacher as storyteller than the preacher who is distanced from both the life of the community and the stories of the tradition. This style of impersonalism also discloses that the preacher is distanced from himself or herself. The Word-event of biblical preaching is precluded when the style of the preacher is alienated from life and its stories. The alternative is a style of preaching which reflects human experience. "Sermons are becoming less formal, more open to the moment, more spontaneous" (*JCB,* p. 24). And this revolution in style is more than a matter of syntax and grammar since for such expressive activities as preaching, style is more crucial to meaning than content.

This question of style, moreover, is not restricted only to the sermon itself. An exciting interaction emerges between worship and preaching when the preacher/liturgist relinquishes the old stereotyped roles.

> We are interested not so much in the polished, formal, finished piece as in the real event which is made possible when a person has carefully and prayerfully prepared something to say, and himself or herself to say it, and then has joined us in worship with the willingness to be really present at prayer and celebration with us even *while* preaching among us (*JCB,* p. 24).

Within the framework of this expressive style, the way that the preacher approaches Scripture is affected as much as the actual sermon itself. Several distinctive characteristics of biblical interpretation, for Rice, relate to an expressive style of preaching.

1. Exegesis is mainly an imaginative kind of listening to the biblical text. The tendency in preaching is to turn too quickly

to commentaries, homily service suggestions, and to "points" and sermon titles. Preachers want to talk before they listen. Specifically, *"we do not do the kind of listening that enables form to spring from what is experienced"* (*PB*, p. 103). The listening that leads to an expressive style in preaching involves a kind of open and expectant meditation on the passages of Scripture. Although the details of this exegetical listening are not elaborated, Rice does emphasize that an awareness of the form of the text is one essential outcome. That form will be closer to life than the various conceptual forms of the old topical preaching. This exegetical listening to Scripture evokes more imaginative sermonic forms.

2. Exegesis is also a kind of seeing of the text by which the preacher imaginatively enters into its world. What is seen in particular are the images, symbols, and stories present in the pericope. "If we have an *experience* of the text," Rice states, "allow ourselves to be led deeply into its images—in our mind's eye to *see* its people, places, and things—to experience its language as a new dawning, there is every likelihood that the resulting sermon will, in form and content, rely upon and awaken imagination" (*PB*, p. 104). There is a need for the preacher to live in the image and story world of the text. This imaginative participation in the biblical symbol is as critical to preaching as imaginative listening, since it results in a coalescence of the world of Scripture and our world. "Image evokes image, story calls forth story, life speaks to life" (*PB*, p. 104). The ability to grasp the symbols of Scripture, which thereby allows authentic vision of our experience, is essential for preaching.

3. Beyond listening and seeing, successful exegesis involves a constant movement back and forth between the biblical world and the contemporary world of the preacher. Rice reminds his readers of the disastrous results of a lack of interaction between Scripture and present experience. "The student who does not learn how to move in both directions is very likely to produce a sermon that imposes contemporary categories and issues on the text or, conversely, a sermon that

confuses exegetical information with gospel preaching" (*PB,* p. 105). What is needed exegetically is this skill in moving between the tradition and experience, much as a ferry moves constantly back and forth (Rice's metaphor). Therefore, if the student or preacher is skilled in biblical studies, the need may be to grow in the interpretation of self and of culture. On the other hand, the person who brings to preaching a deep interest in the contemporary situation will need to develop skills related to biblical interpretation. The goal, for Rice, is not a "then-now" dichotomy, but an interpenetration of the biblical and contemporary worlds possible only through this imaginative listening and seeing.

When the minister who has ferried between tradition and experience stands before the congregation, it is as a storyteller that he or she communicates the Word. Since both the biblical and contemporary worlds have their origin and authenticity in story, their coalescence in the Word-event of preaching will involve the telling of story. But before that can occur, while preachers are in the process of becoming storytellers again, Rice notes the significance of all this for the one who preaches. Past role models for preachers have focused on the "giants," for whom preaching was sort of a feat or performance. Not only had the sermon become stereotyped, but the preacher's personality, too, tended to be defined by the formalism and impersonalism of topical preaching. For preaching to become authentic and biblical, however, this role of "pulpit prince" needs to be abandoned in favor of "a new personalism" in the pulpit (*ESP,* p. 42). "We are seeing the desacralizing and humanizing of preaching," Rice proclaims (*JCB,* p. 24), and the simple activity of storytelling is what is allowing women and men to be more authentically expressive. And as a pleasant by-product of this humanization of the pulpit, the content of sermons is more secular and their delivery is more energized (*PS,* p. 184). Story is the prime homiletical model with regard to both the exegetical process and the critical formation of the preacher as an expressive person. Storytelling is the essential tool for interpreting the tradition, but it is also the means of humanizing the preacher.

By way of summary, Rice states: "No method, in my experience, is more effective in making that connection between the person and the sermon-in-community than the simple art of storytelling" (*PS,* p. 194).

If the homiletical model of storytelling has significant implications for the role of the preacher, it is also of great importance to the nature of Christian community. The purpose of preaching is to enter into a shared story with the community of faith. Without that shared story, the basis for Christian life together is eroded; "an acute sense of brokenness, unreality, and frustration ensues" (*ESP,* p. 31). At the root of the alienation of the community from its tradition, and from itself, is the same pathology—the Story which is constitutive of community and which, through its manifold stories, makes for authentic relationships has been lost. On the other hand, it is precisely the community and its experience which are essential for a recovery of biblical tradition. For Rice, "the preacher as storyteller is a person whose words come as gifts from the community" (*PS,* p. 195). The experience of the community is indispensable. When united with the stories of the tradition, sermonic forms which convey the gospel result. Because these stories, or metaphors, emerge from the actual life of the people, they are in opposition to stories which are "canned" or thought up in the pastor's study. There is a power in the lived experience of the community, evoking genuine images, metaphors, and stories. In comparison, conventional sermon "illustrations" are stories that only ornament; we are used by the stories of the community, while the others we manipulate (*PS,* p. 194). An antidote to this misuse of stories is an authentic involvement of the preacher in the experiences of his or her congregation. Rice favorably quotes one of his students: "Preachers, it would seem, need to live their lives like other people and *then* to make something of it."[7]

One implication of this analysis, Rice suggests, is that the congregation should somehow be more involved in the preparation of the sermon. The people have a significant role to play in preaching, and a small group setting may provide the context for a kind of "communal exegesis" which can best shape and inform the sermon. Such gatherings "can actually provide the preacher with the images needed to lead the larger congregation into an encounter with the text in the Sunday sermon" (*JCB*, p. 26). The renewal of preaching, then, involves a reconsideration of the tradition, the contemporary world, the preacher's style and identity, and the quality of Christian community, all within the homiletical model of storytelling. Only when that model has displaced the old topical, discursive style of preaching is it appropriate to turn to specifically methodological considerations.

What is clear, though, is that for Charles Rice, the forms which the sermons will take cannot be derived from an outlined organization tied to a projective/discursive style. The listening, seeing, and moving which are essential to preaching within a storytelling context result in "more imaginative, free-form ways of putting sermons together" (*PS,* p. 195). And while these sermonic shapes will be freed from any prior rationalistic ordering (points and outlines),. the result will not be a vague formlessness. In many cases, the form of the sermon will be derived immediately from the biblical text. For example, if the biblical passage tells a story, then the preacher may assume some sort of sermonic form in which that Bible story gets told. On the other hand, great stress is laid on the significance of the stories and images found in the experience of the community. These latter sources will similarly provide formal clues as to the ordering of the sermon since in the case of both Scripture and experience, context will determine form (*PS,* p. 194). "What we look for in homiletics today," Rice concludes, "are forms for the gospel that derive from what the gospel is, how it is communicated, and what God in Christ intends for our specific human communities" (*PB,* p. 101). As a sort of homiletical afterthought, an emphasis on the need for homiletical forms is provided which echoes the maxims of the old topical preaching. There is a need for sermons to be "honed" and "disciplined." "In short, the preacher who aims at nothing hits it."[8]

Sermons which are born from an intimate relationship with Scripture and experience will derive their style and shape from inside the framework of a homiletical model of storytelling. Within this range, Rice sees three major alternatives within which the storytelling sermon may take shape. These options, elaborated more recently by Rice from a metaphorical perspective, constitute the major methodological expressions of preaching as storytelling.

1. Metaphor interprets metaphor without explanation. In this approach, the contemporary story-metaphor is presented as the sermon and is not specifically related to the Scripture lesson which has been read. Rice's sermon "Ordinary People," in *Preaching Biblically,* is exemplary here: the Judith Guest story/screenplay is told as the primary metaphor which is allowed to stand in conjunction with a pericope from the Sermon on the Mount (Matt. 6:19-34) (*PB,* pp. 11 ff.). The hermeneutical challenge inherent in this methodological option is the identification of a contemporary story which is congruent with the meaning of the biblical text. Rice stresses the need for careful and extensive exegetical work in the formation of a sermon utilizing this form.

Without such an exegetical foundation, the contemporary story may reflect a portion of the biblical text, but totally miss other equally central aspects. Or, the modern metaphor may introduce a series of issues which are irrelevant or even antithetical to the theological meaning of the pericope. "Ordinary People" is offered by Rice as an example of the effectiveness of this approach based on thorough exegesis and sound biblical interpretation.

2. Allow interplay between lesson and metaphor. Such an interaction is linked with the inductive method of Fred Craddock as well as with the method utilized in many cases by Rice's mentor, Edmund Steimle. Typically, the contemporary situation offers an issue or image which is then expanded and related to the biblical witness. As such a sermon progresses, the contemporary and biblical images interact in such a way that "metaphor and lesson merge into each other and issue in theological reflection and practical application" (*PB*, p. 107). These primary metaphors may be augmented by secondary ones from Scripture or experience, as was the case in the first alternative, above. In neither instance, though, is such elaborating viewed as "merely anecdotal." The secondary images or stories would derive from the same expressive style of engagement with text and experience as the primary metaphors. And it is often the case that such sermons can be reduced to one biblical lesson and one metaphor (*PB*, p. 107).

The "Sermon for Pentecost Day" (pp. 32-37) is illustrative of this approach which engages biblical and contemporary metaphors in an interplay. There is one dominant contemporary metaphor, the story of Rose and Enrique in *El Norte*, and there is one dominant biblical story, that of Pentecost. However, in the interchange between these stories, several other metaphors are offered which elaborate the significance of this interaction. The restaurant image, which in the first place is a sequence within the story of Rosa and Enrique, is expanded into a metaphor of the world which offers hope to' them, taunts them, and uses them. The metaphor is intensified when the activities on the various floors of the Dutch hotel's restaurant are portrayed. Rice takes us on a culinary descent into hell while describing the Hotel Excelsior. The preacher has now provided an imaginative context for reflection on the interplay of the dominant biblical and contemporary stories. But it is important to note that the Excelsior reference is not specifically a story. It serves more fully the function of a metaphorical image as utilized by Buttrick and Vannorsdall. In the "Sermon for Pentecost Day," Rice is utilizing biblical and contemporary stories (the Pentecost account and *El Norte*) as well as biblical and contemporary images (Joel's prophecy, the Excelsior, and the Upper East Side restaurants).

3. Derive the primary metaphor from the Bible itself. Since the biblical text will often provide an image or story that is sufficient as the imaginative basis of the sermon, a preacher may be compelled to simply elaborate that metaphor. The preaching of the black church, Rice observes, almost invariably utilizes this alternative. Here, the Bible is allowed to be "a book of imagination" whose language and stories can be experienced with power and feeling (*PB*, p. 108). In the first alternative, the intersection between Scripture and contemporary experience occurs in the congregation's imagination with little explicit suggestion by the preacher as to its shape. In the second alternative, the intersections are presented overtly in sermonic form. In this last alternative, however, the intersection occurs as the congregation's issues and stories are located within the biblical Story. The locus of this interaction, for black narrative preaching particularly, is found within the world of the biblical stories.

The forms sermons will take, then, are not to be determined prior to the kinds of engagement with tradition, contemporary world, self, and community implied in the homiletical model of story. "The shape of the sermon will vary with the lesson and the commanding metaphor, and necessarily so, since what is required is that the particular language, the concrete images, be heard and seen" (*PB*, p. 108). For Charles Rice, the goal is "holistic preaching" which integrates "the preacher, the listener, and the message in the context of a Christian community" (*PTS*, p. 15).

Evaluation

Preaching as storytelling has much to commend it. When compared to the arid scrubland of topical preaching, the advent of the preacher/storyteller is like a sudden shift to a rain forest. Things are green and growing here. Viewed from the perspective of Sunday morning, the values of the method Charles Rice is advocating are immediate and apparent. People listen, and in many cases are hearing afresh the biblical witness. Story speaks to story, Rice observes, and when that happens, not only can worship come alive, but a whole community of faith can be enlivened. At a more foundational level, a major asset for preaching as storytelling is the rapidly expanding research into the nature of biblical narrative. Particularly as a consequence of recent literary-critical scholarship, the homiletical model of story is now grounded in some of the most evocative and insightful analyses of Scripture in recent years.[9] Storytelling is increasingly being established on hermeneutically firm foundations.

When the movement is made, however, from a recovered appreciation of the art of biblical narrative to a storytelling method of preaching, there are several serious areas of concern which cannot be ignored. To its critics, storytelling, particularly as exemplified in Charles Rice's approach, has a number of liabilities:[10]

1. The limits of storytelling may be defined primarily by the limits of story in the Bible. Not all Scripture is of a narrative literary form even though it may be possible to speak of the stories which constitute the Story. The same literary-critical interpreters who have analyzed the nature of biblical narrative have also identified a multitude of other literary forms in Scripture, such as sayings, poetry, hymns, and theological/convictional systems. The problems for the preacher in all this focus first on the question of biblical preaching on non-narrative texts. Will the new preacher/storytellers limit themselves to a homiletical canon composed chiefly of Bible stories and texts with strong images? Something like this has long been a vulnerability of black narrative preaching and a similar outcome may indeed be the case here.

Other questions as to this method's adequacy challenge story's exclusive ability to convey meaning. Simply put, this criticism questions whether a preacher must specifically deal in story in order to proclaim the gospel effectively. An image, for example, may homiletically fulfill all of Rice's norms regarding the interaction of text and lived experience and still never be expanded into story form in the sermon. Rice has already demonstrated the power of image in relation to story, in "Sermon for Pentecost Day." Considerable research is needed as to the way story and image function to convey cognitive and affective meaning, but it is already apparent that story is not the only appropriate homiletical medium for biblical preaching.

2. As employed by Rice along with the other advocates of preaching as storytelling, there is a vagueness regarding the hermeneutical model of story. In the earlier writing of Charles Rice, the understanding of story was consistently presented. More recently, Rice has used "metaphor," "symbol," and "image" almost interchangeably with story as he has elaborated his method.[11] The result of this elaboration is a new lack of clarity at the center of the storytelling project. To suggest that story is "extended metaphor" is both reductionistic and confusing. Crossan, for example, in *The Dark Interval*,[12] analyzes story with reference to a number of formal categories, only one of which (the parables) involves extended metaphor. Whether from the perspective of a biblical literary critic such as Crossan or from Paul Ricoeur's philosophical inquiries into the nature of language, the equating of story, image, and metaphor is highly problematic. This observation is not intended to restrict Rice to the hermeneutical model of story. Rather, it is to suggest that the addition of such models as metaphor, image, and symbol needs to be made with conceptual precision and clarity. Furthermore, it may be the case that the introduction of a "metaphorical theology" will significantly alter Rice's homiletical method. At any rate, the vagueness of these various models introduces a certain methodological confusion.

3. Issues related specifically to the homiletical method implied in preaching as storytelling also present difficulties for Charles Rice. Between developing the implications of story for an understanding of tradition and experience on the one hand, and portraying three homiletical options for storytelling on the other, he fails to draw attention to the sermonic methods appropriate to preaching the story. This lacuna in Rice's system calls for attention, particularly since an increasing number of preachers have loosed their ties to the old homiletic and have been attracted to some sort of storytelling approach. What is needed now is a "handbook" based on the homiletical model of story in which the methodological implications are fully explored. The problems caused by the present unavailability of such a treatment

of methods are twofold. First, there is a recent trend to elaborate stories within a topical sermonic system. These usually serve as extended illustrations or even function as quasi-Scripture when used as introductions. Obviously such a misuse of story would be appalling to Rice, yet in lieu of a clear methodological option, many preachers have simply retooled their discursive approach, putting more emphasis on the illustrations. Second, for those preachers who have thoroughly grasped the revolutionary character of the story model of homiletics, there is an even more crucial need for explicit methodological analysis.

Given the three different options for preaching as storytelling, Rice is obviously attracted to the first, wherein story interprets story. His "Ordinary People" is exemplary of this approach. But of the three alternatives, the first may be the most difficult to achieve for most preachers and may be personally dismissed as "good for Rice but not for me." However, this exclusion is specifically refuted by the author. Again, a more thoroughly explicated treatment of the methodological implications of storytelling is warranted, especially since preaching the story may come more easily to some than to others. If storytelling is at the heart of the vocation of all preachers, however, a more detailed road map of the path from projective/discursive preaching to the sermon as story needs to be provided.

A SERMON FOR PENTECOST DAY

Charles Rice

JOEL 2:28-32 (RSV)

ACTS 2:1-21

The movie is as complex as that troubled isthmus to our south from which Rosa and Enrique make their way to what they imagine will be the freedom and plenty of life in *el Norte,* the United States. Their godmother in the Guatemalan village of San Pedro, who has been reading *Better Homes and Gardens* for years, tells them of the land of

> private cars,
> > electric kitchens,
> > > and flush toilets.

But it is not for this that the brother and sister leave their village on the dangerous journey through the mountains, across Mexico, and finally to Tiajuana and the border.

Their father, a man who long after his death appears to Rosa in her dreams as a man bringing baskets of flowers to his children, has attempted to organize the peasants who work the coffee plantations, land which had belonged to them but is controlled now by powerful families and their military henchmen.

The father is killed, his severed head hung from a tree, and later the soldiers come for the rest of the family.

Having seen their mother hauled away in a military truck—our tax dollars could well have bought it—Rosa and Enrique make their escape, but not before Rosa goes to the church before daybreak to light three candles, for her father, her mother, and her village.

They are both befriended and exploited as they make their way north. The milk of human kindness flows in the most unexpected places:

A truck driver who menaces everyone on the road, but gives them a ride;

The "coyote" who gets them across the border and to Los Angeles;

A woman in the sweatshop where Rosa finds work;

An emergency room doctor and a patient teacher of English. Enrique finds a job in a three-star restaurant, learns enough English and savoir faire to move up from busboy to assistant waiter.

He is very proud the day one of his elegant customers says, "May I have some more coffee please," and he is able to reply, "Some more coffee? Why yes, of course."

The fact is that Enrique and Rosa do not find freedom and plenty in *el Norte.* They watch from the run-down motel, the maid's room, the waiter's corner, the affluent life around them.

Without papers and money they are constantly vulnerable, helpless to realize their dreams.

They have entered the country by crawling for miles through an abandoned sewer pipe, and they are unable to rise above the powerless subculture of illegal aliens which is tolerated only as cheap labor.

Enrique's father had told him: "To the rich, my son, we are only a pair of arms to do their work."

The mother and father continue to be with them, in their dreams and delirium;

mother is in the motel kitchen, tossing tortillas,
  just as she had the last
time they had supper together on that bloody night
  in San Pedro;
father in the garden gathering flowers for them.

And they continue to burn candles before the Virgin and to pray the prayers of their home.

But it is not enough: the "luck" they hope for does not come.

Rosa has a raging fever, delays going to the hospital for fear of being sent back to Guatemala and certain death, and dies of typhus from the rats' bites. Enrique is betrayed by an envious fellow worker, flees the restaurant by the back door, and the last we see is holding up his arms to a would-be employer: "Look, I have strong arms! Take me! Take me!"

Today is the day of Pentecost, when we celebrate the birthday of the church. That morning, as Enrique and Rosa were fleeing for their lives, they stopped high on the mountain trail for a last look at their home. There, in the center of the village, its role as ambiguous as its facade is imposing, is the white adobe church.

In the movie we see no clergy, and the people come to the church only to bury their dead.

This probably does not reflect accurately, or even fairly, the present role of the Roman Catholic Church in working toward social justice in Central America, though there is the suggestion, as the people sit in a tight circle round the graves of those killed by the death squad, of the rising, and powerful, "people's church" in which the gospel comes to light among those who find solidarity in their opposition to injustice.

But, as the movie shows it, neither in Guatemala nor in Los Angeles is the church there for Rosa and Enrique and their people.

Again, this does not show what many North American Christians are attempting to do for those who have been hounded from their homelands by the repressive oligarchies of Latin America.

All across the United States churches have put themselves on the line in providing sanctuary to these homeless, powerless people, for whom being returned to their countries would almost certainly be the equivalent of Hitler's trains to Dachau and Auschwitz.

We should, even as we seek ways in which we might help the Rosas and Enriques who continue to seek refuge in *el Norte,* be proud and grateful for our fellow Christians who have opened their churches and homes and have, in many cases, gone to Central America to make their witness for justice, some at the cost of their lives.

But the fact is that we are complicit,
    as a church,
        as a powerful, consuming nation,
            as a social class,
in the alienation from their land—in two senses of the word—and in the displacement and suffering of the poor of Central America.

Our government continues its support of oligarchical, privileged groups, while making official protest when the death squads act in behalf of those interests.

El Norte is, in fact, the lavish restaurant in which Enrique works, its excesses of self-indulgence made possible only by the unrewarded labors and, indeed, by the suffering of the poor.

"May I have some more coffee, please."

"Why, yes, of course you may."

The Hotel Excelsior, in Amsterdam, has large windows fronting on one of the canals.

If you stand on the opposite embankment, you can watch the hotel's operation on three levels, like one of those beehives with windows that let you see a cross section of life.

On the hotel's third floor, the managers sit at their desks in well-appointed, spacious rooms.

There are numerous telephones, and now and then the men and women move in and out to confer about one thing or another.

On the second floor, directly below the managerial suite, is a lovely dining room:

 soft light and beautifully dressed people,

  linen, candles, flowers,

   a piano which we can imagine is being played

    just right,

    graceful, courteous waiters,

    people taking their time,

all a veritable symphony of enjoyment.

Most of us would find being there delightful.

On the lowest level, near the water, is the kitchen.

It is organized bedlam:

 chefs pound meat,

  stirring sauces, opening and closing oven doors, yelling at each other while shaking skillets and rolling pastry. The guy madly cleaning fish is drinking wine right from the bottle! And upstairs, not a hint that anyone is dimly aware of what is going on below!

But they are down there, these Rosas and Enriques.

However little we may give thought to them, they are increasingly aware of us, of the world of *Better Homes and Gardens.*

Where, would you say, is the church in this picture?

Who would go so far as to say that the church, particularly the church in our country, is in solidarity with the poor?

Where would we like the church, our church, to be?

Miss Liberty, in New York's harbor where she has welcomed the immigrants who were your forebears and mine, is getting a facelift these days.

We can hope that when the scaffolding comes down she will be resplendent, and that her torch will burn more brightly than ever, to welcome the tired, the hungry, the poor, those longing to be free.

But our real hope today is for the church, that a new birth might come, a new spirit this Pentecost, that what the prophet Joel foresaw for his suffering people might come to all our sisters and brothers, in this hemisphere and throughout the world:

that none will go hungry, even as none will suffer the loss of humanity that comes with having too much;

that none will live in fear, even as none will have reason to oppress a sister or brother;

that people of many races and languages will, by the spirit of God, find their unity.

Joel sings of these hopes:

You shall eat in plenty and be satisfied,
   and praise the name of the Lord your God
   who has dealt wondrously with you.
And my people shall never again be put to shame.
You shall know that I am in the midst of Israel,
and that I, the Lord, am your God and there is none
      else.
And my people shall never again be put to shame.

And it shall come to pass afterward,
   that I will pour out my spirit on all flesh;
your sons and your daughters shall prophesy,
   your old men shall dream dreams,
      and your young men shall see visions.
Even upon the menservants and maidservants
   in those days, I will pour out my spirit.

This will come, will it not, by the spirit of God, the liberation of

all God's people, beginning with the liberation of the church from everything that holds it down,
   that keeps us back from letting go,
      giving up,
simplifying so that we could know the joy of those who with Jesus take the part of the outsider, the outcast, the powerless, the needy. It must come, it can come, to the church and to each of us, by God's spirit.

On the very night that we saw the movie on New York's upper east side, we went quite by habit to a jazzy little cafe for a late supper.

Pasta for two, cucumber salad with walnut dressing, some wine, a piece of chocolate cake and coffee: $41.50.

In paying for it we didn't have to worry even about something so distracting from this scene of beautiful people, perfect lighting, nice food as *money:* it was all handled by plastic, pleasure and power in one little card.

But we all know, and those of us who follow Christ should know it at some deep level, that this is at the expense of millions of Rosas and Enriques, and that their dreams,
      their fathers' and mothers' visions,
of simple human joys established in a world of justice, are also ours.

And so we pray, come, Holy Spirit.

NOTES

1. Edmund A. Steimle, Morris J. Niedenthal, and Charles Rice, *Preaching the Story* (Philadelphia: Fortress Press, 1980), p. 12.

2. Charles Rice, "Shaping Sermons by the Interplay of Text and Metaphor," in *Preaching Biblically*, ed. Don M. Wardlaw (Philadelphia: Westminster Press, 1983), p. 102. (Hereafter *PB*.)

3. Charles Rice, "Just Church Bells? One Man's View of Preaching Today," *The Drew Gateway* 49, no. 3 (Spring 1979), p. 22. (Hereafter *JCB*.)

4. Charles Rice, "Preaching Today: One Man's View," in *Reading, Preaching and Celebrating the Word*, ed. J. Paul Marcoux and Joseph P. LoCigno, (Palm Springs, Fl.: Sunday Publications, 1980), p. 19. (Hereafter *RPC*.)

5. Charles Rice, "The Preacher as Storyteller," *Union Seminary Quarterly Review* 31, no. 3 (Spring 1976), p. 189. (Hereafter *PS*.)

6. Charles L. Rice, "The Expressive Style in Preaching," *The Princeton Seminary Bulletin* 64, no. 1 (March 1971), p. 39. (Hereafter *ESP*.)

7. Charles L. Rice, "The Theater and Preaching," *Journal for Preachers* 8, no. 1 (Advent 1984), p. 21.

8. Charles L. Rice, "Chronicle of a Sermon: Word-Event as the Theological Integration," *The Drew Gateway* 41, no. 3 (Spring 1971), p. 173.

9. See, for example, Robert Alter, *The Art of Biblical Narrative* (New York: Basic Books, 1981).

10. See Richard Lischer, "The Limits of Story," *Interpretation* 38, no. 1 (January 1984), pp. 26-38.

11. "The extended metaphor or story form presupposes the adequacy, indeed, the indispensability, of narrative or image to carry meaning" (*PB*, p. 106).

12. John Dominic Crossan, *The Dark Interval: Towards a Theology of Story* (Allen, Texas: Argus Communications, 1975), pp. 57 ff.

2

HENRY MITCHELL

Narrative in the Black Tradition

The majority of sermons preached in mainline American churches are dull, lifeless, and incredibly boring, according to Henry Mitchell. This preaching is far removed from the lives of the listeners: it trades in argument and concept. At its root lies a syllogistic model of communications. "The dullness of most mainline preaching is due to its being conceived of as argument rather than art—as syllogism rather than symbol."[1] Ideas are arranged in a certain order by the preacher and then transmitted from the pulpit to the people. This dominant approach to preaching, with its rationalistic norms, is identified by Mitchell as "white preaching."

White preaching is the approach found in mainline white Protestant churches and taught in their seminaries. It is not restricted, however, solely to the pulpits of predominantly white congregations. As used by Mitchell, the designation refers to any preaching which is devoid of life and beholden to a homiletical model based on argument. It can occur, and regularly does occur, in black as well as white churches. Ironically, this sermonic norm of the majority church really reflects "an academically oriented counterculture to the folk idiom of America's majority."[2] Its approach to preaching is that of an elite minority within the American church.

The primary difficulty with the rationalistic preaching of the white churches is that it profoundly misunderstands the complex processes of human personality as well as the nature

---

Henry Mitchell is Dean of the School of Theology, Virginia Union University, Richmond, Virginia.

of biblical faith. Preachers have long considered preaching a matter of reasoning with people. The rational consciousness, however, is "that aspect of personhood least capable of all-out belief" (*RP,* p. 154). Information can be offered through such a rational appeal, but faith is different from cognition. Faith involves the whole person and all of his or her faculties.

The human personality is much more than rational consciousness. Persons are emotional beings as well, with intuitive faculties lying far below what is available in the consciousness at any given moment. These emotive and intuitive aspects of a person are "less rational but equally valid processes" (*RP,* p. 12). And preaching, if it is to appeal to the whole person, must appeal to both the conscious and subconscious, to the emotive and intuitive as well as the rational. Mitchell asserts that reason does, however, serve important functions in communication and understanding. First, it serves as a "gatekeeper," monitoring out nonsense received through our experiences. Second, reason provides the language of faith, the language of systematic theology, and the creeds of the church. And third, it serves a vital organizing function related to the experience of faith.[3]

What rationality cannot do, though, is provide or evoke faith. "Faith occurs in the intuitive faculty"[4] and preaching will be most effective when it relates to the intuitive. Given this intuitive locus of faith, rationality also cannot by itself move one to faith. Emotions are involved at all levels of decision-making, especially all the levels of religious decision. And contrary to the liberal dogma that persons are controlled by rational argument, the emotive level of experience is determinative of human actions. There must be a wholeness to preaching, therefore, which addresses all of the aspects of human personality. Preaching must relate to content as well as experience, and most especially to the deepest needs and longings of a person. "Deep must call unto deep—personal depth speaking to personal depth" (*RP,* p. 152).

From the perspective of black culture and experience, however, any assessment of personhood which is delimited to a scrutiny of the individual is inadequate. There is as well a collective or communal dimension to the so-called "unconscious" dimensions of human experience. As defined by Carl Jung and Mircea Eliade, "the term *collective unconsciousness* has real meaning and relevance in the interpretation of Black culture and its communication" (*RP*, p. 15). Mitchell prefers the term "transconsciousness" to speak of this "culture-borne religious life," which is in fact "a kind of stored *insight*" (*RP*, p. 16). This transconsciousness is transmitted primarily through oral communication and forms the medium within which a culture's religious symbols and values endure. The genius of black preaching has been its ability to transmit these traditions effectively and thereby relate to persons at a transconscious level of experience. This style of preaching, which involves all aspects of human personality and draws on the power of transconscious religious symbols, comes to its fullest expression in the black narrative sermon. It is this understanding of preaching as story within black culture which is "the wave not only of the past but of the future" (*RP*, p. 24).

At the heart of the oral tradition within the black church is the "transgenerational transmittal of the originally oral traditions which we now know as the Old and the New Testaments" (*RP*, p. 24). These sacred writings were transmitted orally in the beginning, and the task of preaching is to restore them to their original character as the story is retold. Whatever else the Bible is to the black church, it is story, and whatever can be said about black preaching likewise involves storytelling. At a more general level of cultural transmission, "plays and stories are processes which engage the vital emotions, making possible new understanding and a new orientation and commitment."[5] But more specifically related to that oral tradition which is the church's "transconsciousness," the depths of human experience have been reached best by a retelling of the Bible story. Faith is evoked at its most profound biblical level by narrative preaching which addresses the whole person within her or his cultural context.

In order to probe the working of biblical narrative and to explicate its profound power, Mitchell has turned most recently to an analysis of the patriarchal narratives of the Old Testament (*PP*, pp. 36 ff.). Why is it, he asks, that God has placed the medium of saga or folk tale at the heart of the biblical tradition? Why do we not find instead theological statements proclaiming eternal truths? The answer, for Mitchell, "lies in how tales impinge upon consciousness" (*PP*, p. 37). They do not direct their appeal solely or primarily to the rational consciousness—which is significant in a negative sense since Mitchell denies to the latter a decisive function regarding faith and volition. The saga, even in its most primitive form, however, is able to achieve what the most sophisticated argument cannot. It is able to "have an impact upon the total person, and especially the intuitive sector of consciousness, wherein dwells faith" (*PP*, p. 37). Consequently, the secret of the power of the patriarchal narratives lies in their ability as tales to provide a vicarious experience of the truth. Persons may then more readily appropriate that revelation since they have in some sense already lived it.

The psychological power of saga, Mitchell observes, derives from this potential for inviting the hearer into a vicarious experience of the deepest levels of truth.

> What psychiatrists call levels of trust cannot be argued up; they are planted and watered by a vast and complicated array of experiences, both conscious and unconscious, actual and vicarious. . . . However, actual experience is diffuse and unfocused, while vicarious experience can be quite purposeful. When I identify with the prodigal son well told, I may learn/experience as much in twenty minutes as might have taken twenty months or many years to "walk out" on the ground (*PP*, p. 38).

When a Bible story (such as a patriarchal narrative) is retold in preaching, this potential for profound vicarious experience is made available to the hearers. And that experience can have an impact at every level of their personal and communal existence.

To probe biblical narrative for the "secrets" which provide for focused vicarious experience is to offer as well the generic outlines and logic of narrative preaching. Mitchell will argue that the genius of black preaching has been its faithfulness to these actual characteristics of biblical story while clothing story in the distinctive and congenial environment of the black cultural tradition. The patriarchal narratives, for example, gain their power by virtue of "the details of personalities, the description of subjective response . . . and, above all, meaningful conversations" (*PP,* p. 40). Narrative preaching at its best, then, will draw on these elements of the biblical story to provide an "eyewitness" account. Fleshed out in ways appropriate to a people already at home within an oral tradition culture, the black narrative sermon becomes the fulfillment of the Bible story's original intention. The saga continues: "The teller relives the tale in all its vividness, and makes available to the audience a vicarious *experience* of the theological theme projected by the inspired editor's use of the sources" (*PP,* p. 40).

The black Bible is story. It is the story of God's gracious and merciful actions on behalf of a covenant people little deserving of such compassion. Within the context of this account, the most significant truths related to human existence are not portrayed as objective, rational propositions. Rather, they are couched in narratives which have the capability of speaking to the whole person, providing for an intuitive level of apprehension and behavioral appropriation. But this power of biblical narrative can only be communicated if the story is retold effectively and from an "eyewitness" perspective. For Mitchell, "all that has been said about the Black Bible involves or implies storytelling" (*BP,* p. 132). Some preaching in the black tradition, he admits, will be topical in nature, but the best will transmit Scripture's insights within a sermonic context most immediately congruent with the Bible. Methodologically, this preaching "is likely to issue forth as the exposition of a text of scripture" (*BP,* p. 112). However, for the black preacher, it will need to "issue forth" most specifically and repeatedly as storytelling.

Simply put, the central challenge for a black preacher is to *"learn the art of telling a Bible story meaningfully"* (*RP*, p. 35). The question is asked implicitly and explicitly of every black preacher, from seminarian to retiree: "Can he [or she] tell the story?" "It is probable that the one skill which above all others can open the door to influence and service [in the Black church] is the skill of telling the story in the dramatic, imaginative Black idiom" (*BP*, p. 133). For some, the tradition is received by cultural osmosis combined with a personal gift for the art. Other preachers may have to labor at developing these skills, particularly if they have been significantly affected, homiletically, by their experiences in a predominantly white seminary. In any case, the dynamics of black storytelling can be identified, organized, and celebrated. The beginning of this process for Mitchell is the transformation of the preacher into a storyteller.

Preaching is an art, and as such is dependent upon the skills of the narrative artist. As a prior condition to effective, dramatic preaching, therefore, the preacher must be the first to vicariously experience the biblical saga. Implied at this point is a bifocal emphasis on the most profound range of human experiences: "one both has some deep experiences of one's own, and one appropriates others, chiefly from the Bible" (*RP*, p. 35). In the latter arena, an internalization of the biblical story must occur in order for the action and the experience to be authentically recreated. Mitchell would admonish any prospective preacher-storyteller: *"Very careful study is required to get enough real facts to do an honest work of biblical art in an eyewitness account*—a masterpiece of the transconscious communication of a tale, if you please, from the Holy Bible" (*RP*, p. 35). Such study is especially critical with respect to the setting and characterization within the biblical story. The elaboration of these two factors is the litmus test of true black preaching.

This research cannot, however, be the end of the matter for the black preacher. As the biblical story is investigated, a probing of the preacher's own experience also becomes decisive. Stated firmly, *"one cannot generate a rerun of an experience one has never had personally nor appropriated"* (*RP*, p. 34). Initially, this means that the preacher must know his or her own story and be able to see how it relates to the biblical saga.

> One's depths cannot cry out a message or conviction never lodged in those sacred precincts in the first place. To proclaim truth transconsciously one must possess it likewise, or at a gut level. I find myself telling preaching class after preaching class that sermons must come because the depths cry that they have something to say, and not because it's their turn and they have to say *some*thing. . . . It is a waste of time to try to help a person build a sermon about anything that is not deeply his or hers (*RP*, p. 34).

This capability of relating "transconsciously" is dependent upon a prior exploration of the depths of the preacher's own experience.

On the other hand, the black storyteller is compelled to know, and vicariously to participate in, the personal and communal experiences of his or her people. A people are drawn into community by the collective, transconscious apprehension of a shared story and a shared tradition. And the black sermon functions as an important vehicle for the transmission and celebration of this story. Here again, the preacher will be especially attentive to the *personae* of the black story, since these characterizations will be crucial for the necessary eyewitness perspective. "The Black preacher must be up to his ears in the condition of his people, and out of this comes the easy dialog between people whose lives are intimately close together—so close together that the themes which invade the consciousness of the one also invade the other" (*BP*, p. 104). Not only must the preacher make his or her own the rich spread of biblical story, but also through the crucial "tapes" of personal and communal experiences involving "great truth and deep feeling" (*RP*, p. 37).

The ability to create a vicarious experience of the biblical story is dependent upon the art form of characterization. If the lessons of the Bible story are to be taught, there must be an identification with the characters who originally learned them or embodied them. The experiences of these persons "will be profitably relived, however, only if the *details* attract the listener to move into the stream of experience of the tale" (*PP,* p. 41). One cannot become an eyewitness when the details of setting and characterization are inadequate or remain vague. Such detailing within the sermon becomes the bridge for the hearers to cross into the world of the biblical saga by providing "the tiny commonalities between ancient and modern life" (*PP,* p. 41). If such details are present within the scriptural text, it is essential that they be identified and well communicated in the sermon. More often, though, there will be only a suggestion of such detail, and the preacher will be tempted to "make do" only with what is given. For the black preacher, Mitchell observes, such a meager approach is seriously inadequate. Elaboration is needed as an essential component of oral rendition. "Where there are no details, one must use inspired imagination to put back into the record what was dropped out as unessential to the main issue" (*PP,* p. 41). Like milk which is dried to make it portable, but which needs water to become drinkable, the biblical story needs creative elaboration to be experienced vicariously. Immediacy and vividness are needed for such eyewitness accounts, and the preacher's challenge is to recount and/or elaborate the story in such a way that it can be relived today. Hence, Mitchell concludes that these biblical materials are used when there is an elaboration of details in harmony with the source, and of rendition or performance which amounts to a "rerun" of the experience (*PP,* p. 40).

A second major component of black narrative preaching is highlighted when Mitchell states that "to vivid detail must be added effective timing" (*PP,* p. 41). There is tension and suspense in the biblical saga, and these must be "carefully and patiently built, with clear awareness of the exact conflict" (*PP,* p. 41). This sense of timing is essential to any good storytelling, but it is particularly valued within the black tradition. Here, the goal is not simply the employment of a story for a "point," but as the occasion for a vicarious experience of the biblical message. Such a participatory mode of communication necessarily will take time to deliver and to be received. Mitchell enthusiastically endorses Gardner C. Taylor's observation: "Emotions take time" (*RP*, p. 43). Given this insight, the black preacher may begin the sermon in an almost understated manner, and in most cases the delivery will be slower than is the custom in white preaching. "Black Bible stories," Mitchell notes, "are to be relived, not merely heard" (*BP*, p. 139). The movement of a biblical narrative is toward a climax in which there is experienced a profound truth—in short, a revelation. The same movement obtains for the black narrative sermon. Whatever else is expected in black preaching, in addition to the story's presence itself, a sense of timing and climax must be evidenced. There must not be a premature disclosure of the climax of the story, nor must there be an anticlimax or lengthy conclusion following the relief of the suspense (*BP*, p. 142). While the sermon may move the hearers along a number of hills and valleys, the expectation is always present that at last the journey will conclude on the mountain top. Here, the significance of vivid detail is most crucial, since a depth of participation in the story must be provided for hearers in order that a fitting climax may occur. This sense of an ending, though, is not limited to a question of timing. As Mitchell observes, "once that denouement was arrived at, it was *celebrated*" (*PP*, p. 41).

The climax of a black sermon is most properly a celebration of that which has been "joyously given [and] received" (*RP*, p. 55). Its uniqueness lies in the "feeling tones" which come to expression between preacher and people. "The Black climax, at its best, is a kind of celebration of the goodness of God and the standing of Black people in his kingdom, as these elements have been expressed in the message" (*BP*, p. 188). Mitchell stresses that the celebrative climax is to serve as a reinforcement of the material provided within the body of the sermon. The issue at stake must now grip the people, but no new issues should be added. "The hearer is permitted to relax a bit from reaching after new spiritual insight, and to lift up in confirmation and gratitude what he has already received" (*BP,* p. 188).

This expressive and healing celebration is one of the most valuable aspects of black preaching, Mitchell would argue. Celebration fulfills several key functions related to the sermon and the community: (1) It is a "reinforcement for retention and availability" (*RP,* p. 55); (2) It serves to affirm the personhood and identity of the hearers "by means of free expression, which is accepted in the religiocultural context" (*RP,* p. 56); (3) It enhances a sense of community among the hearers; (4) It provides "a habitable 'living space'—the establishment of a celebrative island of consciousness in an ocean of oppression and deprivation" (*RP,* p. 57).

While no new material should be added at the climax of a black narrative sermon, there are some notable characteristics of the rhetoric of this closing which confer its celebrative tonality. The language itself should partake of celebration, which, for Mitchell, implies a shift from German to Latin-derived words.[6] Frequently, the celebration is worked by a use of hymn texts or Bible stories drawn from the community's oral tradition. Specific elements of the black rhetorical style, such as intonation and a more rhythmic pattern of speech, may become more evident as the climax builds to celebration. Mitchell finds a shift from objectivity to subjectivity, however, to be essential for the emergence of this climactic celebration. The black preacher will shift from a third to a first person account and speak of the experience at issue in ways both intensely personal and yet kerygmatic. Testimony, and not objective fact, is the mode of expression of such a climax (*BP,* pp. 188-89).

A third major element in the black preaching style is dialog. There is a call and response pattern to black preaching which necessarily invites the participation of the hearers. "The Black worshipper does not merely acknowledge the Word delivered by the preacher; he talks back" (*BP,* p. 44). Mitchell adds: "Sometimes the Black worshipper may shout" (*BP,* p. 44). This response is a sign of the sense of expectancy conveyed through authentic preaching within a black context. And it is a sign of the worshipers' sense of acceptance, of being at home. But for Mitchell, such dialog is also an indication that preaching has moved beyond the intellectual exercise seen in most white churches. While the responses of the people do indicate an acknowledgment of the truths received from the sermon, they signify as well that the preacher is speaking to the deep-felt needs of the congregation.

Dialog as an aspect of preaching in the black church functions in several significant ways for Henry Mitchell. These contributions of dialog both underscore the validity of the analysis of the intuitive and tranconscious dimensions of black culture as well as the effectiveness of black narrative preaching in addressing these depths. First, dialog must be initiated or stimulated in order that a more general participation by the worshipers may occur. Preaching that is dialogical needs to begin as dialog if it is to end in dialog. "A dull, incommunicative start may establish a pattern or structure, a relationship between preacher and congregation which cannot subsequently be changed" (*BP*, p. 110). A second role of dialog in black preaching is the establishment and/or expression of a kind of intimacy between preacher and people. Dialog functions to disclose the congregation's "close rapport with the speaker" (*BP*, p. 110). The initiation of this dialog "says to the hesitant and the uncertain that it is safe or acceptable to open up to the Spirit that is present through the preaching of the word" (*BP*, p. 110).

A final role of dialog involves the more expansive dimensions of this free expression and self-disclosure. This "opening up to the preacher is only a part of a larger opening up to God and the group as a whole" (*BP*, p. 110).

> In a hostile white world, [Blacks] have had to be close-lipped and poker-faced to survive. Because they have been of necessity such great actors and self-concealers, they do not readily respond to any therapeutic formula which requires self-disclosure. And yet there must be some place where Blacks can actually open up and let out feelings safely. The Black Church has been that place (*BP*, p. 111).

Authentic dialog in black preaching, therefore, is profoundly healing and cathartic. There is a freedom granted in
black worship which allows the full range of human emotions
to be expressed in God's presence, from the greatest joy to a
healthy purging of "guilt, sorrow, pain, and frustration" (*BP*,
pp. 45-46).

In addition to the central elements of black preaching—
characterization, climax, and dialog—a number of subsidiary
aspects of black style are identified by Mitchell. Most of these
qualities relate to the three elements which have been
identified as most crucial to the success of the black sermon.
What should be noted, however, is Mitchell's insistence that
with regard to stylistic concerns, there is a remarkable
permissiveness within black congregations, who will accept a
wide variety of expressions "unrelated to the message" (*BP*,
p. 162). Nevertheless, the following elements of rhetorical
style have gained a rather normative standing as belonging to
the etiology of the black sermon.

1. Intonation. This most common and stereotyped of the
mannerisms in black preaching involves the use of a
chant-like musical tone (*BP*, p. 163). Whatever else intonation serves to convey, Mitchell views as its most pervasive
function the signaling of a kind of black identity. Originating
in the African custom of sung public address, it is fully
understandable that the preservation of such intonation in
black preaching would remain as "an affirmation of Black
identity, a means of celebrating and supporting Black
personhood" (*BP*, p. 165). The more specific functioning of
intonation beyond its use as an "identity signal" relates to the
enhancement of the sermon climax. Mitchell does note,
though, that many black congregations apparently no longer
need intonation as an essential element of climax and
celebration. Nevertheless, intonation is an effective means of
expressing the depth of a climactic experience grounded in a
solid context (*BP*, p. 166).

2. Black English. The black sermon may utilize intonation
and accent, but its blackness is more fully expressed through

the black English dialect. Mitchell lists three important advantages to this use of familiar dialect:

> In the first place it presents the message in a familiar and authentic folk-art form, and attracts attention by giving pleasure and making folks at home or more comfortable. Secondly, it reinforces and supports Black identity by putting in the mouth of God the language of the people. . . . Finally, the message is made much more understandable by the use of familiar language (*BP*, pp. 155-56).

Distinguished from standard English by a slower rate of delivery and a somewhat simpler sentence structure, black English is most commonly associated with a drawl. The latter, Mitchell adds, is not "by any means a universal characteristic of Black speech" (*BP*, p. 158). Another widely perceived feature of black English is the use of unmatched subjects and verbs. Here, too, Mitchell cautions against a stereotypical identification of black English as involving "bad grammar."[7]

3. Repetition and Rhythm. Repetition is not only present within the call and response rhetorical elements, but within the general course of the sermon as well. "Texts, aphorisms, and other significant statements are restated for emphasis, memory, impact and effect" (*BP*, p. 168). Within the context of the black church, such repetition is received mainly as an indication of the worthiness of the dialog and of its context. Such repetitive material, Mitchell observes, may be retained by the hearer well after the sermon has ended, because of the vividness of its impact. Interestingly, the element of rhythm is not seen by Mitchell as nearly so important a dimension of the black preaching style. Most white observers, "including folklorists as well as anthropologists and theologians," focus on a perceived rhythmic element in black preaching closely related to the use of intonation (*BP*, p. 166). Yet Mitchell's own research does not support these claims. He does allow that breath patterns within an intoned portion of the sermon may make for a somewhat rhythmic effect. In general, though, he underplays this element of black style. Mitchell concludes that "while rhythm is vitally important in Black music, it is, to say the least, unimportant in Black preaching" (*BP,* p. 167).

4. *Rhetorical Language.* While there seems to be at present a white commitment to "dour, barren language" in preaching, the black church still values a rhetorical beauty in preaching. Such language does not result in more complex sentences, however. Such poetic language is couched in relatively simply and easily remembered sentences. Still, this linguistic embellishment is not viewed as mandatory within the black church, although more "rhetorical flair" exists there than within white, middle-class congregations. "Perhaps it would be accurate to say," Mitchell concludes, "that *one* of the many strengths of good Black preaching is the skillful use of poetic rhetoric" (*BP,* p. 174).

In addition to these prevalent elements of black style, Mitchell notes several "lesser features" which, nonetheless, are found in black preaching. Aphorisms, he observes, are used more frequently by the black preacher than by his or her white counterpart. Also, he asserts that "the response of the Black audience to aphorisms is much greater than is customary in other churches" (*BP,* p. 176). Another less frequently employed aspect of black style is the stammer or hesitation. Such a feature builds suspense at important points in the sermon, but serves also as another cultural signal. The one who stammers is seen as groping for God's truth: an image of weakness is conveyed with which the congregation can identify (*BP,* p. 176). And what is true of such hesitation obtains for every element of black style. These preaching techniques are indigenous to black culture and oral tradition, and all serve to enhance the sense of identification and solidarity between preacher and people.

Finally, Mitchell offers some more general methodological considerations which relate at some point to the vesture of black narrative preaching. In keeping with the admonitions of past generations of homileticians, Mitchell adheres to a "main idea" locus of sermon organization. "If real communication rather than a show of erudition is the goal, one good idea will be a quite satisfying achievement" (*RP,* p. 43).

However, this orthodox wisdom is immediately qualified when the writer adds: *"If you have an idea that can't be translated into a story or a picture, don't use it" (RP,* p. 45). The latter advice shifts the context of the sermon to at least a well-illustrated topical approach or, more probably, into a fully narrative model. In the latter case, Mitchell cautions against breaking the narrative character of the experience. "Avoid stepping out of the tale to give interpretative or technical asides, not even chapter and verse" *(PP,* p. 40). The eyewitness approach to storytelling must be presented consistently and with clarity of focus. And once in the story, the preacher-storyteller should have as the goal that climax where the gospel is celebrated and the people find release.

Evaluation

Henry Mitchell is an able preacher and a faithful commentator on the black homiletic tradition. He has performed a vital service for the black church in particular and for all other preachers as well through his thorough studies of the history of black preaching. As an investigator and interpreter of this vital tradition, Mitchell has become an important influence for the transmission of the values of narrative preaching in the black church. However, he serves not only as a "social anthropologist" of the black pulpit tradition, but also as a vigorous advocate for its recovery on behalf of the renewal of the whole church. When the church settles into a rationalistic, argument-oriented style of preaching, Mitchell invokes the past tradition of preaching in the black church as the way toward a recovery of effective proclamation. Particularly for the black church, the affirmation is made that its essential identity and mission will persist only by virtue of a persistence of the values expressed through an oral tradition centered in the pulpit.

Through his writings and lectures, though, Henry Mitchell is also serving as a constructive homiletician at several key points. First, he is seeking to integrate the insights of depth psychology and social philosophy in order to more fully interpret the power of narrative in Scripture and in proclamation. His rejection of a "liberal" anthropology—and with it, liberal preaching's rationalism—is based on a vision of human wholeness that involves affect and volition as well as the intellect. Mitchell is accurate both in his critique of liberalism's inadequate anthropology and in his assessment that faith is a function of the affective and volitional aspects of personality. Secondly, Mitchell is providing a more constructive contribution by exploring a hermeneutics of biblical narrative and by relating those findings to homiletic method. Choosing the patriarchal narratives as the locus of his investigations, the analysis of the function of saga in human consciousness and Christian tradition is of positive benefit in overcoming the heightened then-now bind brought on by historical-critical method. Finally, Mitchell's constructive work involves his critical stance toward the black homiletic tradition. Not all expressions of black preaching are seen as of equal value, and some applications of the tradition can constitute actual misuse. So, as a black homiletician and preacher, Henry Mitchell is best fitted to insist that the various expressions of black pulpit rhetoric be utilized in service of the biblical message and the needs of the congregation. He understands precisely how the power and effectiveness of these rhetorical elements may tempt the preacher to ignore the hard struggle of elucidating a clear message from the text.

The other side of this coin, however, is that in his dual role as reporter and constructive homiletician, Mitchell has ably commended the variety and sweep of black preaching's expressive style. There are some surprises in his findings, as, for example, when he observes that intonation and rhythm are not nearly as ubiquitous in black style as is normally assumed. The former relates most specifically to the sermon climax, while the sense of rhythm involves the far more pervasive dynamic of call and response (*BP*, pp. 166-67). Closely related to these investigations into black style are Mitchell's findings on the formal characteristics of black narrative preaching. "The power of the art," Mitchell discovers, "is located in details of characterization, descriptions of subjective response, and especially in significant conversations" (*PP,* p. 40). Based on these narrative elements of the patriarchal tradition, several extremely helpful suggestions are recommended for any preacher attempting to "preach the story." While that crucial sense of timing which evokes celebration may be more "caught" rather than "taught," it is normative for black narrative preaching and is appropriately emphasized by Mitchell. His other suggestions are of more immediate applicability, including the importance of remaining in the story without interruption and the need for great attention to detail in personality and setting. These lessons are of importance for every preacher who is faced with the joy and challenge of preaching within a narrative style; but Mitchell insists that they be learned well by anyone called to preach within the black church.

Shifting from a celebration of the black preaching tradition and Mitchell's constructive homiletics to a more critical stance, two major issues need to be identified and discussed. The first relates to the tradition itself to the extent that it tends to focus on the narrative aspects of Scripture at the expense of other literary forms. In some cases, the motto "Preach the Story" has functioned more as a principle of scripture selection, "Find the Story." That is, the preacher's choice of biblical passages for preaching may become inordinately restricted to mostly narrative literature, resulting in a black homiletic canon of the Old Testament narratives, the prophets, the Synoptics, and the book of Revelation. While the rest of the biblical witness is also read and preached in the black church, there may be more resorting to a topical, argumentative approach when the story is not already given in the text. At any rate, one of the issues for the evaluation of any homiletic method must be its adequacy in dealing with most, if not all of the Bible. Biblical preaching is weakened to the extent that a specific approach to preaching is significantly oriented more toward one type of biblical literature than another.

A second issue focuses on the homiletic norm of a main idea which Mitchell invokes from time to time. Here, as with other homileticians explicating an essentially narrative system, he seems to need to retain an ideational principle of control over the sermon. Interestingly, neither Mitchell nor his narrative companions (Rice and Lowry) want to retain a rationalistic hermeneutics. Yet when the homiletic method is elaborated, Mitchell sees the need for a kind of thematic sermonic control which was not evidenced within the biblical narrative. Particularly for an interpreter who celebrates the multiple meanings of a narrative as contributing to its depth, this "single point" sermonic caution seems to work at cross purposes. In fact, given the value of the close congruence between Mitchell's hermeneutic and homiletic methods, this insistence on an ideational sermonic focus becomes the striking exception. All of the other aspects of hermeneutic and homiletic method, as described by Mitchell, dovetail rather nicely. It may well be that the notion of plot as explored by Lowry and Buttrick can serve more effectively as the principle of control in both the narrative pericope and the sermon's own sense of movement and structure. If that is the case, then a main idea orientation may prove extraneous to any of the live options in homiletic method.

THE PROVIDENCE OF GOD

Henry Mitchell

GENESIS 50:14-21

I want to talk to you this morning about an interesting thing, and I say interesting because in Black culture the Providence of God is far and away the most popular doctrine. Most people might not know that they had a doctrine and certainly there's never been such a thing as a popularity contest about doctrines. But there is no real mystery about why this is so popular both in Africa and in Afro-America. This is something I have stumbled upon in recent years and, in fact, am in the process of writing a book about: these doctrines, these affirmations keep people alive.

So I want to spend some time talking about the affirmations that have kept Black folk alive. In the process of writing, I am with a psychiatrist-type; we are showing how these affirmations keep people alive. The clinic in which we have road-tested these affirmations is in a posh place called Newport Beach, California. So we find the total spectrum of humanity that wishes really to live whole and abundantly must have a belief system to support that sort of thing. We can perhaps be accused of proposing something that might be called "affirmation therapy," because we are dead sure that people who have an adequate belief system in most cases won't even need to see our clinic. In fact, Black folk made it this far through the unbelievable tortures and absurdities of oppression in this country without any clinical help at all, largely because they had a belief system that made it possible for them to cope. And that belief system has universal applicability, and is, to be sure, out of the very heart of orthodox doctrine, as one might call it.

I suppose the best expression of this doctrine is to be found in Romans, the eighth chapter and the twenty-eighth verse, where Paul says that God works in everything for good to those that love him and are called according to his purpose. Everything works for good for those that love him and are called according to his purpose. Two very simple propositions. God works in everything. There is nothing that happens that does not somehow fit into either the direct will or the permissive will of God. God knows about it all and God gives permission. Nothing happens outside what is known and permitted by God. And in the last analysis all that happens can be by the power of God and providence of God made to be for good.

It sounds simple, but most of the time we don't really think about it. It is probably more alive in our unconscious or in our intuitive than it is in our conscious minds and we don't even think about providence except in extreme joy and extreme sorrow. So I want us to think about it now, and perhaps resolve to deal with it so deeply that our own lives will be changed. God works in everything. He works in all aspects of life. God, as Jesus put it, has counted the very hairs on your head. Nothing is too tiny. Some years ago my wife and I were working on doctorates—at a Methodist school by the way, the School of Theology at Claremont. As you know, graduate student apartments are not terribly large, and I used to clean house occasionally. I'm the housekeeper in the pair. And I discovered a tremendous number of hairs on the floor, and I could tell they weren't hers. I used to wonder why I was not bald, in the light of the number of hairs that would collect over a period of two or three weeks, whatever the intervals between cleanings were. And it dawned on me one day that Jesus had said—whether I'm bald or not—that God knows everything including the number of hairs on my head. Jesus said he knows about even a sparrow who falls, and they're only worth a half a penny. God knows about it all, God works in all of it, and this is of extreme importance to all of us.

We live in a culture where people are busy now engaging in a lot of things that seem not to take this into account. I think in particular of—what do they call that stuff—astrology. People ask me, When were you born? I say in September. "Oh, you're a Virgo." And that means so and so. And this is fine for conversation purposes, you know everybody has some kind of a sign, and if you want to converse, that's one way to break in. But please, for God's sake don't take this business seriously. Can you imagine me coming before the judgment seat of God saying: sure I've done it, God, of course I've done it, but you got to understand I'm a Taurus and Tauruses does it like that! This is heresy, to put it mildly, and this has been long known. Even back in Jeremiah the word is out—don't be watching the stars and the heavens and astrology because this is what heathens do. God has it all in his charge, or her charge, take your pick, and we live therefore a kind of protected existence regardless of what we see. Regardless of how bad it may look. God works in everything and God guarantees that we are protected. This is no new idea, not only in the Bible, but in Black culture and in some other cultures. I marvel when I look at what happened with slaves who were being oppressed beyond our imaginations. The "Roots" saga on television did not dare tell it like it really was because even as it was, a lot of people got sick. In the midst of all of that, here are folks singing from the bottoms of their souls, "He's got the whole world in his hands." Utter spiritual genius to know that in the midst of this absurd injustice God has the whole world in his hand and this can only be because in African culture the Providence of God and the omnipotence of God were old hat. We didn't learn that from a man with a whip in one hand and a pistol in the other. We learned that from our African ancestors and it was so deeply embedded in our culture that it gave us the momentum to carry us through centuries of torture and bring us out singing, "He's got the whole world in his hands." I well remember back about 1939 when Marian Anderson was scheduled to sing a concert in the hall of the Daughters of the American Revolution and then it was determined because of her ethnic identity that this should be cancelled and one of the great moments of my life was to look on the Movietone News and watch her singing, "He's got the whole world in his hands." She wasn't singing in the auditorium to those few thousand, she was singing to many, many more thousands outside under God's heaven. And singing with a triumphant lilt in her voice, God has the whole world in his hands. And God is working in all for good, even if you lock me out. But look at how many more people I'm singing to now. Now, of course, this could sound to some very thoughtful folk like wishful thinking. It could appear that, well, this is the sort of thing you hold on to just to keep from going crazy but, I mean, it's just a dream. And I would readily consent that it is possible that some people do it like that. I would never suggest that nobody can prove that it is wrong. Slave ancestors would have told anybody who had challenged them that you just haven't watched it long enough; in the last last analysis it will work for good.

I would suggest three kinds of good and they begin with *L's*. I love alliteration. God works for good in the limits, the leavings, and the last end. God sets a limit on how much can be brought against any of us, so that we can always bear it. God clearly sets a limit, just as God set a limit on Satan in the trials that were permitted to come to Job. God said thus far and no further. And for all of us who live in the midst of perplexing problems—and Blacks have no monopoly on perplexity—God has set a limit and there is always that profound conviction that life will not get out of hand. God sets a limit and then God is provident also in the leavings. There are people, you know, who look at a glass and say it's half empty. Those are pessimists. And if they look at it and say it's half full, they're optimists. The point is, there is always something left. Many years ago I went to hear Dr. Martin Luther King, Senior. Very much like Howard Thurman when he wanted to say something really profound, it was usually something his mother or grandmother or some ancestor had told him. And that's something to think about; those ancestors had some very powerful insights. King said his mother told him to always thank God for what was left. And that was something to think about because, you see, if you've got enough breath left to complain, you do have something left.

I thought that was very impressive, and I really made a mental note of it. Some years later, I went back to Atlanta, to Ebenezer Church, and by this time Dr. King had lost A.D. and M. L. and his beloved wife had been shot to death right before his eyes at the organ stool in that very sanctuary, and guess what old man King was saying: "Thank God for what's left. There's always enough left in life to make it worth living." The providence of God guarantees that you should never stop the world and get off, there's always something left to live for.

Thank God for what's left, for God is provident in the limits set and in the leavings and, for purposes of alliteration—the last end. Life will always come out right. Many years ago I heard an English Baptist evangelist who had preached I guess a thousand time a sermon called "Murder the Ump'!" This sermon was a parable of baseball, and with the World Series just concluded it's quite appropriate at this moment. What he said in that sermon about the "ump' " was very impressive but it set afire in my mind a totally different idea, namely, that life is like a world series: all too often it may appear that the hosts of hell are getting the edge, but if they got a million runs you must understand, it's only the first inning. When the game is over, you will discover that all along it was a "fixed" game and whosoever you are, wherever you are, whatever has happened, God still guarantees that the kingdom of this world will become the kingdoms of our Lord and of his Christ. Our entire lives are staked on that certitude.

As I close, I am reminded of what could be the testimony of a man named Joseph. And it's very interesting because this testimony, as one finds it in Genesis 50, is in the very early years of Hebrew thought. This is not something that came along in the years of positive thinking. This is something that was really seminal to the whole of the development of Hebrew faith. We all know of course that Genesis was not the very first book written, but obviously Genesis comes to this marvelous conclusion, this great climax: "You meant it to me for evil, but God meant it to me for good." It's a very powerful story.

The older brothers were headed back to Egypt where they had left their flocks and their families after they had buried their father in the old family burying ground. They were talking about what Daddy said. Daddy said, "You know, Joseph has been nice to you because, well, he didn't want to worry me. But once I'm gone he's not going to have me to inhibit his vengeance. I would strongly suggest that you go to him and make peace because that was a heavy trip you got laid on him." They heard this warning and they knew that it was well founded and they sent a word ahead and got an appointment with little brother Joseph who was also, it happened, the prime minister of Egypt. And then they went to see him and they made the same speech that in effect they had given in the request for the interview. They said, "Little brother, we've come to tell you that we're sorry for all that has happened. We've watched you as you've come through all this and you've come through admirably. You went off to slavery and you refused to be compromised. You were unjustly accused and you had to do a stretch in Pharaoh's prisonhouse. Instead of this embittering you, you somehow made of it a ministry. Now you've gone on to be Prime Minister and this has not turned your head; indeed you have been gracious unto us. But like Daddy said, we know that you must have done some of this so Daddy wouldn't be upset and now that he's gone, we feel like a chicken running in an open field before a hawk. It's just a matter of time." Then they fell down on their knees and they begged his forgiveness and said "We are your servants." Joseph all the while had been crying. He was deeply moved by all this and he said, "Get up, don't treat me like a god. Yes, I know how evil you were; I know very well that you narrowly escaped putting me to death. I know that you sold me into slavery, and I know that there is nothing more vicious than the competition, the hatred, the hostility that exists sometimes between blood brothers. But even though all of this happened, you must understand that while you meant it to me for evil, God reserved the right to bring good out of it. So I'm the Prime Minister today, and I am gladly and willingly capable of feeding a lot of people including yours." He could very well have said in our terms that God works in everything. "He didn't want me to be a slave, but he reserved the right to squeeze out of even that atrocity a blessing. God works in everything for good!" When you believe like Joseph, you can hold on and keep whole no matter what happens. Amen.

NOTES

1. Henry H. Mitchell, "Preaching on the Patriarchs," in *Biblical Preaching: An Expositor's Treasury,* ed. James W. Cox (Philadelphia: Westminster Press, 1983), p. 37. (Hereafter *PP.*)

2. Henry H. Mitchell, *The Recovery of Preaching* (San Francisco: Harper & Row, 1977), p. 11. (Hereafter *RP.*)

3. Henry H. Mitchell, "The Recovery of Preaching" (lecture delivered at Duke University Divinity School, Durham, North Carolina, October 17, 1984). Mitchell adds that reason serves also to provide "intellectual curiosity."

4. Ibid.

5. Henry H. Mitchell, *Black Preaching* (New York: Harper & Row, 1979), p. 133. (Hereafter *BP.*)

6. Mitchell, "The Recovery of Preaching," Duke lecture, 1984.

7. *BP,* p. 158. See pp. 158-61 for his discussion of the contrasts between standard and black English.

3

EUGENE LOWRY

Narrative and the Sermonic Plot

As viewed by Eugene Lowry, the problem with preaching is
that it has adhered to a spatial paradigm for its self-understanding. Within this paradigm, ideas or propositional truths
are the components of the sermonic whole. The traditionally
taught homiletic, with its "three points and a poem,"
necessarily impels the reader "toward organizing sermons on
the basis of the logic of their ideational ingredients.[1] Treating
the sermon as a "thing," the traditional task of the preacher
became the shaping of the sermon's conceptual space.

Inevitably, this paradigm deals in spatial images of
construction—Lowry recalls that he had been taught "the
engineering science of sermon construction" (*HP*, p. 13). The
titles of the most influential books on preaching of the last
several generations clearly reveal this organizational bias. W.
E. Sangster's text of the 1950s, for example, was entitled *The
Craft of Sermon Construction*,[2] but, as Lowry observes, this bias
persists in the present, as indicated by J. Randall Nichols' new
book, *Building the Word*.[3] Beholden to this spatial paradigm,
preachers have long assumed that the project of "sermon-
building" involved fitting together an assortment of ideas.
The spatial model is static, rationalistic, and discursive. Its
central problem, for Lowry, "is that the whole schema is born
of an image of sermon building as *assemblage* which is
founded upon our unconscious understanding of reality as
meaningfully related pieces" (*HP*, p. 10).

Eugene Lowry is professor of preaching and communication, Saint Paul
School of Theology, Kansas City, Missouri.

The Copernican Revolution in homiletics involves an abandonment of this spatial paradigm for one grounded more fully in the biblical witness. This new approach, deriving its method and its power from the story of God's dealings with a covenant people, will need to leave behind most of our "cherished norms about sermon anatomy" (*HP*, p. 5). This more revelatory paradigm relates to time rather than space, and supplants ideational content with story. A sermon, Lowry maintains, "is an *event-in-time*, a narrative art form more akin to a play or novel in shape than to a book" (*HP*, p. 6). Such an assertion implies that preaching involves movement and direction, a journey of some sort with the congregation, and for Lowry, the compass readings for this sermonic trip are taken from biblical narrative.

In his most recent book, Lowry has sought to explicate the full implications of this shift in homiletical paradigms. The "conversion" from the traditional model of space to one of time demands a rather radical realignment comprising several major considerations. These he presents in a series of antitheses:[4]

1. *"The Task: To Organize or to Shape."* The static, spatial image of traditional preaching calls for sermon preparation which both identifies and organizes ideas. There is a serious tension between the two activities, however, since a series of discrete propositions does not necessarily provide coherence or unity. Often, the supposed corrective, a "main thesis" for the sermon, reflects an underlying, prior disunity within the sermon's collection of ideas. "One speaks of *attaining unity*," Lowry correctly observes, "only when one assumes it is not already there" (*DT*, pp. 14-15). Two other problems emerge when conceptual preaching is viewed from a methodological perspective. First, the inherently static quality of proposition-ally stated ideas has made any kind of sermonic movement difficult to achieve. Succinctly put, "Once a proposition is stated, it is done; closure has occurred, and only with great difficulty can one get things moving again" (*DT*, p. 15). This closure is inherent in the propositional model, and is, in fact, its goal. Yet the result is congregational inattention and

disinterest. The second of these problems relates primarily to a theological consideration of the norm of control which informs sermon preparation. Organizing ideas into a sermon, no matter what structure is finally developed, implies a control over the biblical material that may not appropriately belong to the preacher. "The image of ordering ideas assumes a resultant mastery" (*DT,* p. 15). On the other hand, it is more likely the case that preacher and people need "figuring out" and not Scripture. The challenge, therefore, is to listen to Scripture and to shape experience rather than to organize a collection of ideas. But in order for such shaping to occur, the preacher must be attentive "to *movement* rather than *thought*" (*DT,* p. 16).

2. "The Form: A Structure or a Process." Notes for a sermon may resemble either a blueprint or a road map, evoking a sense of vertical assemblage (points) or of horizontal movement. Organizing ideas inevitably leads to a structural sermonic form, while those "who *order experience* and whose task therefore is to *shape* will find their sermon form to be a *process*" (*DT,* p. 17). Moreover, the grammar of the sermon form contributes to this definition as structure or as process. The former embodies "points" which create stasis by virtue of their propositional format. For the latter model, however, the more significant points or events within a sermon convey movement and transition. While sermonic structures are marked by declarative statements, Lowry adds that "a sermon process often will be marked by a question" (*DT,* p. 17). Finally, it is significant to note that in the sermon viewed as a structure, the points or propositions are, in principle, interchangeable. (That is, it matters little whether points about the "inspiration," "preparation," and "anticipation" of faith are in any given order.) Yet in a sermon viewed as process, a readjustment of its sequence may radically alter or even subvert its meaning and intention. Hence, "process road markers are by necessity in series" (*DT,* p. 18).

3. "The Focus: Theme or Events." In the form of a comment on the two prior alternatives, Lowry next draws the distinction between a homiletical focus on theme or events.

The organization of ideas into a spatial structure inevitably brings risk of a focus on a theme. The preacher here is challenged to discover "a unifying ideational thread" (*DT*, p. 19). On the other hand, experience ordered into a process leads to a focus on the events within its duration. The identification of a main thesis is no longer necessary as a controlling principle.

4. "The Principle: Substance or Resolution." At a mostly subconscious level of awareness, according to Lowry, one of two norms monitors our work of sermon preparation. If the preacher asks along the way, "How am I doing?" these alternative norms become more explicit as perspectives for self-evaluation. Closely related to the spatial model is the principle of substance. If the preacher has set out to organize ideas, the issue becomes "Are we getting *it* said?" (*DT*, p. 20). Conversely, an ordering of experience into a process raises more appropriately the issue of destination or, for Lowry, "resolution." Here, the question becomes, "Are we getting there?" Anticipating a later discussion, he adds that such resolution does not come directly or with automatically increasing clarity either in narrative or in preaching. A sermon is not like a car trip! Rather, it is often the case that resolution "increasingly becomes more remote and difficult, *apparently*, until by some strange shift or move the resolution happens with utter surprise" (*DT*, p. 20).

5. "The Product: An Outline or a Plot." Informed by the subconscious moves of substance or resolutions the resultant sermon will be shaped in one of two widely divergent manners. Quite obviously, the formal outcome of an organization of sermonic ideas is the venerable outline, which is "utterly true to the informing image of preaching it represents" (*DT*, pp. 22-23). However, when employed as a device to order experience, the result is unsatisfactory, if not disastrous. There is here "a mismatch of content and form" (*DT*, p. 23). Why an outline is an inappropriate way to order experience becomes evident when it is understood that the ordering of events within a narrative is a function of plot. There is some kind of "sequential ordering" in a plot which typically includes "an opening conflict, escalation or compli-cation, a watershed experience (generally involving a reversal) and a *denouement* (that is, the working out of the resolution)."[5]

   6. *"The Means: Logic and Clarity or Ambiguity and Suspense."* The goal of an outline is logic and clarity; it is a systematic means of organizing ideas. To state that the values of logic and clarity are the criteria for preaching is to deal explicitly with an ideational context. Within such a field, "the question of cognitive coherence is central" (*DT*, p. 24). A plot, on the other hand, has as its means ambiguity and suspense, and the question becomes one of correspondence (is the plot "real" to life?) rather than coherence. In order for suspense to be maintained within a sermonic plot, the test is "whether ambiguity based on discrepancy is maintained successfully until the preacher is ready to resolve matters with the gospel" (*DT*, p. 24). Lowry then concludes that

> often what is "good" for the outline is "bad" for the plot—and vice versa. For example, clarity of purpose in an outline is considered important and should be presented in some form in the introduction. But if it is ambiguity you are trying to maintain, you certainly would not want to let the cat out of the bag. Likewise, ambiguity is often taken for imprecision by followers of the outline method. What is appropriate is utterly dependent upon the informing image of one's work, whether ordering ideas or ordering experience (*DT*, p. 24).

   7. *"The Goal: Understanding or Happening."* It is strange, Lowry notes, that there is no evident consensus among those who regularly preach as to the goal of preaching. But it is even stranger, he adds, that the division here is not grounded in a theological orientation. Rather, this division over homiletical goals is "between those whose sermons appear to place highest priority on cognitive conceptualization and those whose sermons do not" (*DT*, p. 25). The latter group, of course, includes those preachers who order experience and will thereby move toward the goal of some sort of happening. These divisions follow neither theological persuasion nor

ecclesial tradition. The preacher will have as his or her goal either understanding or happening, depending on the basic paradigm being used, along with its respective norms. Fundamentally, again, the question will turn on whether the preacher operates from a model based on space or on time.

Which side of the issue Eugene Lowry espouses is hardly a surprise. Given the choice between understanding and happening, he chooses the latter with enthusiasm, and likewise for the categories of experience, process, and eventfulness, and centrally for the choice of time over space. This is, in fact, his central thesis: "The sermon is not a thing at all; it is an ordered form of moving time" (*DT*, p. 8). Against this assertion, the sad reality is that many preachers who preach out of such a perspective are thwarted by the drag of preachers' "collective unconscious." In spite of this implicit influence of organizing ideas, Lowry observes that "when we do well in the pulpit often it is when we lay aside our outlines of space and begin talking to our people in time" (*DT*, p. 27). If one defines the sermon as an "event-in-time," the next question addressed to Lowry by the outline-bound preacher is simply, "What is time?"

Initially, Lowry answers by negation—time is not space, and any preaching which attempts to organize ideas "tends to stop the clocks" (*DT*, p. 29). Those preachers, therefore, who traffic in "timeless truths" render their sermons lifeless since the congregation both listens and lives in time. Similarly, the preacher who uses a "method of distillation"[6] is not only isolating one element of a scriptural text and treating it spatially but is, more importantly, distilling out time as well. Still, the question persists, "What is time?"

Lowry's analysis of temporality begins with a distinction between outward time and inward time. While he labels the former with *chronos,* the latter is defined as the subjective time of our inner clock. We experience this inner time as duration and find it constantly in tension with outward time. Moreover, in some fashion it mediates our experience of the external world of chronos. "[Inner time] . . . helps determine our capacity to process space-time experiences and in turn is shaped by them" (*DT*, p. 32). One of the immediately apparent difficulties for the preacher which Lowry notes is that within the time of the sermon, "there are as many inner clocks as there are listeners—all ticking at different speeds" (*DT*, p. 32).

Beyond the more obvious categories of outer and inner time, however, is *kairos,* the "right time." Lowry does not see kairos as a third category alongside chronos and inner time, however, but sees it more as an event in time "which implodes two or three other kinds of time" (*DT*, p. 32). Such a kairotic event then, is defined as involving: "(1) . . . an interaction among an exterior event, one's inner time, and chronological time; (2) . . . the sense of duration being temporarily suspended (even unselfconsciousness about time's passing); and (3) . . . some type of profound impact" (*DT*, pp. 32-33).

As interpreted by Lowry, kairos is most fully occasioned by story—not only stories on film and stage, but those of liturgy and preaching as well. By the liturgical reenactment of the biblical story, the worshipers become participants in it, or it becomes contemporaneous with them. Such a reliving of the biblical story evokes kairos, the right time.

An interesting question related to the broader issues of providence and theodicy is raised by Lowry at this point. Are all instances of kairos God's doing, occasions of revelation? Clearly, times of insight or celebration may occur for a person apart from the agency of divine self-disclosure. One must conclude, then, that "kairos may or may not include an assumption about God's activity" (*DT*, p. 34). Another perspective on time is needed when chronos becomes kairos through divine action. This revelatory situation Lowry designates as God's time.

Apparently God will not leave chronos alone, and the Christian community continues to acknowledge the intrusion of God's time upon planet earth. "Whether in the form of Dodd's realized eschatology, Bultmann's existential apocalypse, Crossan's advent of Being or even the Rapture folks' driverless car, they all hold this one conviction in common: *chronos* is not the last word" (*DT*, p. 35). The power of preaching from this perspective is that God does not leave the chronos of the sermon alone, but calls it into question, names it, and transforms it. Every sermon's goal, then, is "to prompt such intersection of God's time with our *chronos* and inner times that the kairotic event happens" (*DT,* p. 35). As Lowry has already argued, though, the homiletical means toward this end involves the ordering of experience within a narrative plot.

Lowry introduces a final aspect of time related to the sermonic potential for kairos. If, as he argues, story is the most powerful context for prompting kairos, then the time within a story, narrative time, must be taken into account. "Picking up *chronos* and *inner,* reaching for *story,* announcing *God's* and praying for *kairos,* narrative time dances in, through, and around all the times" (*DT,* p. 38). In order to understand the sermon as this ordered form of moving time, therefore, the nature of story must be examined in some depth. Through its capability to order time meaningfully, the meaning of life itself is ordered through story. Personal and social longing and identity are best expressed through the medium of story. In fact, it is not clear what would remain of the human condition if there were not stories.

> For we dream in narrative, daydream in narrative, remember, anticipate, hope, despair, believe, doubt, plan, revise, criticize, gossip, learn, hate and love by narrative. . . . In order really to live, we make up stories about ourselves and others, about the personal as well as the social past and future.[7]

If story functions so profoundly to give meaning to existence, and if preaching is to follow the same narrative path, then it becomes crucial to understand the "powerful properties" of stories. Fortunately, the preacher can turn to a whole succession of narrative artists as well as to those who have more formally analyzed the unique character of narrative in both its literary and oral expressions. To assist in appropriating this power of story, Lowry turns to Wesley Kort's work, *Narrative Elements and Religious Meaning,*[8] for an explication of the nature of narrative. Kort focuses on four central dimensions of story—setting, plot, character, and tone. Lowry adds a fifth, narrative time, and expands upon that dimension of story at some length; however, it is necessary first to examine those aspects of the four other dimensions of story which Lowry views as essential to his project of developing the narrative basis of preaching.

1. Setting. The initial function of setting is to locate the lives that we portray in a story. Whether historical narrative or science fiction, setting is a necessary aspect of story which locates the situation in a specific time and a specific place. And by virtue of this location, an important service is provided in surmounting the "abstract-concrete polarity" of oral address. In place of the generalizations frequently dispensed from the pulpit, a narrative system is provided concretion by virtue of its setting.

Lowry underscores a further function of setting, however, which has far-reaching implications for preaching: "The importance of setting in a story . . . is not simply that life is *located*, but that life is *limited*" (*DT*, p. 44). By this is meant the giveness of a story's space and time which cannot be changed, either by the characters, narrator, or the listeners/readers. There is a finitude conveyed through narrative by virtue of the specificity of the story's setting; life is bounded and real (i.e., people do not always get what they want or deserve). In contrast to the limitations given through a story's setting, preaching frequently deals only in the victories of the gospel while ignoring life's pain and tragedy. Not only does such an approach let the cat out of the homiletical bag (by treating resolution before complications), it also "suggests, at least to the more thoughtful, that in fact we may not take the borders of existence seriously" (*DT*, p. 46). If, on the other hand, the sermonic form is story, its element of setting introduces that limitation necessary for both a credible approach to life and an integrity to the response of the gospel.

2. Character. The introduction of a character or characters into a story's setting initiates the disclosure of "the potential of human consciousness to know and manage the world in which it finds itself."[9] By this is not strictly meant the possibilities for existence claimed by the "human potential" movements, but rather the qualities of character which will be called up and challenged by the story. The awareness that conditions and circumstances evoke such radically different responses, though, leads Lowry to join with Kort in speaking of the resultant "paradigms that illuminate the human potential for good and evil."[10] This power of character within story is not only derived from the wide spectrum of human nature which is encountered, but from those expressions of character which uncover almost undefinable aspects of existence. In this sense, Lowry notes, character in story "has the peculiar power to . . . sharpen perception about *how* to think" (*DT,* p. 48). The conscious paradigm presented through characterization evokes our previously held unconscious images of human potential. As this engagement occurs in the midst of story, we may become aware of aspects of human existence already known but hidden, or "we are grasped by a new vision of life we never understood before" (*DT,* p. 49). This illumination of the images of human life is a vital function of character in narrative.

3. Action. Once characters are introduced into a setting, action soon follows. The narrative begins to trace the chain of events which will eventually constitute the story. This much is obvious. What is crucial for preachers, however, is a more sophisticated distinction between action and plot. Hence, Lowry questions whether plot refers to *"incident, action,* or *chain of events only,* or is the term's referent to be taken as including some additional principle or movement?" (*DT,* p. 50) Having written a book explicating what for him are these principles and movements *(The Homiletical Plot),* Lowry restricts his description of action to the former considerations of incident and chain of events. Plot, for him, means something related to action, but more narrative in nature. Also, it is clear that while action happens to characters in a narrative, homiletically, Lowry wants to apply the category of plot to any scriptural text, with regard to the shape of the sermon.

4. Tone. The element of tone might be set aside as a somewhat superficial dimension of story. It could mean only the effect of the story's setting on the listener/hearer. But for Lowry, tone "refers to the work's *created subjective presence*— the world view that stands silently articulate behind the writing" (*DT*, p. 59). Consequently, tone discloses the intent of the narrative artist and her or his world view. Within the scope of a sermon, tone will function in a similar fashion to shape the course of the action, the characterizations, and the setting. Difficulties arise, however, when the tone of the sermon discloses values and judgments which are in tension with the stated homiletical content. This stylistic issue of how a preacher deals with a subject is always significant and may, in fact, speak more forcefully than what is said (*DT*, p. 60).

A further characteristic of tone within narrative art relates to its association with the issue of point of view. The point of view within a story can be that of a character or characters, a narrator, the author, or audience. In the context of narrative preaching, two additional points of view become possible— those of the preacher and the congregation. Note that audiences provide a different point of view from congregations, formally speaking. However, narrative preaching can place the contemporary hearers of the sermon in the place of the auditors of a parable of Jesus, for example, as well as identify them with various characters in the story.

5. Narrative time. Underlying all of these elements and qualifying them is, for Lowry, the factor of time. There is a "facticity of time" (*DT*, p. 61), the medium through which the characters and actions will live. The story is limited not only by its spatial setting, but by its temporal framework as well. And although the narrative artist can be, through flashback and the compression and expansion of subjective time, quite creative concerning the uses of time, there is a "givenness" of time which is essential for story and for life. As such, temporality is the most intimate link between the story's power and the audience or congregation.

When a storyteller invites us into a "world" with its setting, characters, action, and tone, narrative time is also begun. It is the time of the story. And if every sermon is conceived as a narrative, whether or not based on a biblical narrative or parable, a sermon's time is narrative time. By treating every sermon in this way, as an ordering of experience in time, the preacher "will enlist the power of *time* in the preaching of the Word" (*DT*, p. 77). Methodologically, enlisting narrative time, for Lowry, involves an assessment and utilization of the principles of plot as distinguished from the more limited understanding of the element of action. Prior to this explication of plot, though, Lowry distinguishes between an ideational definition of the sermon as spatial, which he rejects, and the ideational dimensions of a narrative sermon, which he affirms.

If the formal basis of the sermon is story, then all of the elements of narrative, including time and plot, obtain for homiletical method. At the early stages of sermonic gestation, though, the preacher may be unclear as to its shape or plot. There are two preliminary stages of preparation which Lowry defines as "wondering thoughtfulness" and "I think I have one." At the first stage, the lections have been read, ideas written down, commentaries and other sources checked, yet not much is known yet about the sermon. At the second preliminary stage the preacher focuses in on the idea which will be formed into a sermon. Moving from the first to the second stage, though, is one of the most difficult challenges in preaching. "How do you move," Lowry asks, "from generalized sermon thoughts to a genuine sermon idea?" (*HP*, p. 18) Recent homiletical tradition, he observes, is of two minds on this question—one either begins with a theme or with a problem. But something is missing from both approaches:

> The first reply concentrates on the substance of the sermon, the central "message" to be preached. But if this is the central priority in our sermon preparation we will tend to produce lecture-type sermons which are strong in content but weak in establishing contact with the congregation. If we follow the advice of the second kind of reply (focusing on problem or felt need) we likely will establish quick rapport with the listeners but be weak in content (*HP*, p. 18).

Clearly, then, Lowry views as unacceptable an approach to sermon preparation from either a wholly conceptual or wholly inductive perspective. What are missing for him are not only the values of the alternative method—that is, both the thematic and situational concerns necessary in biblical preaching—but a form or context within which they can appropriately interact. That form, of course, is given through the narrative shape of the sermon. Lowry concludes, therefore, that "if a sermon is perceived as a *plot,* formed and shaped by the *interaction* of problem and theme, the sermon idea begins to take on life" (*HP,* p. 19). This interaction with a felt need will produce a sermonic idea which will come to full expression as a living sermon through the form of a plot.

The intersection of need or problem and theme presents Lowry's other, more inductive side, which is meant to complement his insistence on the centrality of story. The inductive expression figures in two regulated contexts—at the point of generative interaction and at the normative sequential movements within his homiletical plot. As will be seen with Fred Craddock, the sermon has its origins in "itches" or "scratches," while Lowry's "extra mile" is his insistence that every act of sermon preparation involves both. Hence, "sermons are born when at least implicitly in the preacher's mind the problematic *itch* intersects a solutional *scratch*—between the particulars of the human predicament and the particularity of the gospel" (*HP,* p. 20). The primary clue to the formation of the sermon idea, then, is this tension between problem and theme which offers up a sense of discrepancy and suspense. But when the sermonic idea takes form for Lowry, the roles of need and theme are central to the shaping of the homiletical plot. The resultant sermons "are always problem-solutional" (*HP,* p. 20). The same sense of tension and suspense will be sustained in the sermon through the normative shape of its plot. Every sermon, he insists, should move from need to solution, from "itch" to "scratch."

In order for preacher and congregation to move through this problem-solutional dynamic, it is necessary that the latter risk a significant element of trust in the preacher and in his or her preaching. And it is likewise necessary that the preacher maintain suspense if such trust, or even interest, is to be sustained. "The listeners knowing we are about to lead them down a risky road—hopefully to some resolution born of the gospel—must have the confidence that we are capable of doing the job credibly, convincingly, theologically, and hopefully" (*DT*, p. 66). Only the narrative sermon based on the biblical story can fulfill these expectations and thereby earn this trust. Moreover, only the sermon whose shape is formed by a narrative plot can convey the central ingredients of suspense and ambiguity which can bring the listeners all the way from need to resolution.

Suspense in the homiletical plot—as will be seen—derives its effectiveness through movement from ambiguity to resolution. Inherent within every sermonic plot is a sense of issues and actions not yet disclosed. There is necessarily "the suspension of revelation and decision" (*DT*, p. 67). Yet this essential ambiguity does not mean preaching which is ambiguous as to focus and relevance. Such preaching is vague rather than suspenseful and far removed from the particularities of both the congregation's needs and the gospel's response. If the message is clearly conveyed that *nothing* significant is at stake, congregational trust is lost.

In order to avoid such a loss of trust, preaching must express genuine problems of human existence thrown against the particularity of the gospel of Jesus Christ. Moreover, in its essential form, the sermon is "a premeditated plot which has as its key ingredient a sensed discrepancy, a homiletical bind" (*HP*, p. 21). There are two general kinds of plots which offer themselves for homiletical usage, Lowry observes. A movie plot will typically begin with a felt discrepancy and move to an unknown resolution. Complications thicken the plot as it moves toward its unknown conclusion. On the other hand, a television series plot will begin in a similar manner but move toward a known conclusion (the crew of the *Enterprise* will all be on the next episode of "Star Trek" along with their captain and starship). Sermons, Lowry observes, fall most accurately into the second form of plot, since the community of faith already knows that resolution of the issues of human existence is provided through the Incarnation of Jesus Christ. How the gospel will respond to the particulars of the binds and discrepancies of our lives, however, is the issue open to ambiguity. And for Lowry, "this unknown middle ground provides the context for sermonic tension" (*HP*, p. 23). In order for this movement from ambiguity and homiletical bind to resolution through the gospel to occur, the specific stages of a sermon plot must be identified and appropriated. Lowry defines these stages as "(1) upsetting the equilibrium, (2) analyzing the discrepancy, (3) disclosing the clue to resolution, (4) experiencing the gospel, and (5) anticipating the consequences" (*HP*, p. 25).

SERMON
PLOT

Stage 1: Upsetting the equilibrium. Initially, interest must be created before it can be maintained, and this is best done by upsetting the equilibrium of listeners. Within only a few minutes (two or three) the preacher's itch will need to become that of the congregation, through the introduction of an attendant ambiguity or "bind." Lowry likens this stage to "the opening scene of a play or movie in which some kind of conflict or tension is introduced" (*HP*, pp. 30-31). The preacher is granted an important opportunity within this first stage since the opening tension may or may not relate to the main theme of the sermon. Just as a good story may have several sub-plots and could begin by introducing any one of them, a sermon can similarly begin by focusing on an ambiguity which is subsidiary to the central issue. It is crucial, however, that the preacher not leave a minor ambiguity unresolved when the point for the introduction of the sermon's central bind has been reached. Closure must be given to any subsidiary ambiguities quite early in the sermon. Lowry's advice to the preacher regarding this decision is as follows:

> As a general rule, when a context of a sermon is the contemporary human situation, whether at a personal or social level, it is likely that the opening ambiguity will be the central or fundamental discrepancy. In the case of expository

or doctrinal preaching, it is more likely that the opening ambiguity will serve to engage the congregation in a preliminary bind which in turn opens into the central problem (*HP*, p. 33).

Lowry offers one other suggestion related to this first stage of the homiletical plot. While the resolution of the plot should never be disclosed here, some direction to the ambiguity should be provided. "Undifferentiated ambiguity," he notes, "soon becomes no ambiguity at all" (*HP*, p. 35). Given adequate clarity and direction, however, ambiguity is the sense of the beginning of any narrative and consequently of the homiletical plot as well.

Stage 2: Analyzing the discrepancy. Once the opening bind of the sermon has been disclosed, it can be easily lost through either premature resolution or persistent vagueness. The challenge for the preacher in this second state of the homiletical plot is to retain and even enhance the ambiguity introduced in stage one. Such retention and interest is sustained here by virtue of the sermon's analysis or diagnosis of the discrepancy, a process usually resulting in greater length than any of the other stages. The suspense is maintained during this diagnosis since the outcome is not yet possible or methodologically desirable. Stage two is a time for "diagnostic wrestling—of theologizings"; the congregation's attention is held "because the bind is not yet solved and there is therefore no option but to stay involved in the sermonic process" (*HP*, p. 38). Once a discrepancy has been introduced, it is the preacher's duty to perform sufficiently extensive analysis so that some particular aspect of the gospel responds to something now made equally concrete and explicit. Moreover, this process of diagnosis is crucial since it will determine the consequent form of the sermon, "including the form of the good news proclaimed" (*HP*, p. 37).

The difficulty for preaching, Lowry observes, is that while such diagnosis is crucial for the effectiveness of the plot, in practice it is usually the weakest aspect of the sermon. Rather than engaging in the serious and challenging work of this diagnostic wrestling, many preachers make do with simple description or illustration. Neither will do, however. In the case of the former, the preacher will trade in generalizations concerning the human condition, etc., with the assumption being made that to so label something is really to explain it. On the other hand, illustration is even more frequently invoked as a substitute for analysis. Illustrations, after all, are much more specific than generalized descriptions, and seen therefore as more helpful. Nevertheless, illustrations tend to deal with human life at a behavioral level alone, and rarely disclose, let alone analyze, motives. Treated only from the empirical evidence offered in an illustration, situations and decisions may be conveyed as relatively uncomplicated and unambiguous. Yet the factors underlying the behavioral outcome of a situation may be incredibly complex. The purpose of this analysis, then, is "to uncover the areas of interior motivation where the problem is generated, and hence expose the motivational setting toward which any cure will need to be directed" (*HP*, p. 40).

The need for in-depth diagnosis is also critical for Lowry's inductive approach, since it assumes a principle of correlation between the human bind and the gospel's response. Superficial or nonexistent analysis will result in a gospel response sounding both stereotyped and incredible. The good news will come out sounding like a collection of "poetic answers" to life's little changes. Furthermore, the preacher's role as a theologian demands that the diagnostic task be carried out with seriousness and precision. Homiletically, this process of analysis provides the most appropriate context for testing and refining the theological positions held by the preacher.

Stage 3: Disclosing the clue to resolution. The goal of diagnosis is to provide some sort of explanation and with it some sense of outcome. In our cause-and-effect world, a scientific, medical, or homiletical investigator assumes there is a "missing link" which, when found, will lead from problem to solution, from itch to scratch. The process, however, is not usually one of ever increasing insight and awareness. Rather, a number of possible solutions are scrutinized during stage two and rejected, sustaining suspense—the sense of "bind." And when a clue to resolution is finally uncovered, it is frequently experienced as a surprise, as revelatory. "In gestalt terms, it is the 'aha,' the one piece which allows the whole puzzle to come into sharp focus" (*HP*, p. 48). These clues, Lowry reports, are more "experienced" than "known" by the listeners.

When the clue to resolution is given through the distinctive movement of the homiletical plot, there is typically a reversal of prior expectation. A radical change in direction significantly alters the congregation's sense of outcome, based on the prior analysis. Attendant on such a revelatory experience is often the need to rethink the "common sense" utilized in some of the diagnosis provided during stage two. Consequently, the new and revelatory clue is received as an intuitive leap, turning normal expectations, and the sermon, upside down. As a paradigm of biblical narrative, Jesus' parables consistently embody this principle of reversal and surprise. A hated Samaritan becomes the one who extends mercy and grace. The prodigal son is welcomed home and it is revealed that the older son rejects his father's grace and hospitality.

However, this principle should not only be evident in sermons based on such biblical reversals. The gospel will invariably come as a reversal of human expectations and overturn the consequences disclosed through our analysis of the homiletical bind. In contrast to this principle of reversal, Lowry notes that "the fundamental mistake of the liberal Protestant pulpit of the last forty years is that it presumes that the gospel is continuous with human experience" (*HP*, p. 60). Such is the case, he adds, only after that experience has been overturned by the power of the gospel.

Stage 4: Experiencing the gospel. The ability to experience the gospel through the homiletical plot depends to a large degree upon the success of the analysis provided in the two prior stages of the sermon. By the time the preacher and congregation have arrived at the fourth stage, the bind which provided for ambiguity needs to be explored through insightful diagnosis. Only when such in-depth analysis has occurred are listeners ready to hear the good news of the gospel. Unfortunately, a "homiletical short circuit" frequently interrupts this process; there is often "a giant, and ill-fated leap from the beginning of stage two (analysis) to stage five—which is the stage of anticipating what can or ought to be done in light of the intersection of the problem and proclamation of the gospel" (*HP*, pp. 62-63).

Such short-circuiting not only fails to take life seriously and thereby the gospel as well, but it serves to prematurely release the sermon's necessary tension and ambiguity. The time-oriented sermonic plot loses the control of movement essential to its narrative character.

When the first three stages convey a sense of discrepancy which is then insightfully analyzed, the gospel is heard effectively, i.e., the Word does what it proclaims. This intersection of the specific form of the proclamation of the gospel with in-depth diagnosis of some specific human bind is at the heart of the homiletical plot. All previous diagnosis of the discrepancy has led now to the declaration of God's response in Jesus Christ. Identifying the latter is relatively simple if the prior diagnostic work has been well done. "When I have done my diagnostic homework and the decisive clue has emerged," Lowry states, "the good news has fallen into place sermonically as though pulled by a magnet" (*HP*, p. 65).

Stage 5: Anticipating the consequences. The sense of the ending within Lowry's homiletical plot differs considerably from that usually experienced in conceptual preaching. What marks the conclusion of a conceptual sermon is its character as climax and as call—a sermonic "asking." Within a sermon plot based upon narrative movement, however, the climax comes earlier, in stage three when the reversal occurs, and again when the gospel is experienced in the next stage. The similarity in the two approaches—that an anticipation of the gospel is located in the same relative position as a conceptual sermon's "call"—is really only superficial. Methodologically, the climax in the narrative plot sermon has *already* occurred by the time stage five has begun, and closure is now being effected. This ending is critical to the plot, however, since it explicates the future "now made new by the gospel" (*HP*, p. 67). The preacher now asks, "What—in light of this intersection of human condition with the gospel—can be expected, should be done, or is now possible?" (*HP*, p. 67) Congregations and preachers now jointly consider the consequences of the surprising reversals introduced by the gospel.

There is a second, more theological consideration raised by this comparison of topical and plot endings. Lowry attacks the tendency of the former to make the sermonic climax synonymous with the sermonic call as a form of works righteousness. That theological problem, he claims, is inherent within conceptual preaching's method. On the contrary, the focus of our preaching "is upon the decisive activity of God, not upon us, and hence the climax of any sermon must be stage four—the experiencing of grace through the gospel" (*HP*, p. 69). Our response to that proclamation is important, but is not the center of gravity for the sermon. What *is* at that center is the good news of Jesus Christ. Methodologically, the preacher can call for a response at stage five only because a new *freedom to choose* has been effected through the hearing of the gospel. *"Freedom,"* Lowry asserts, *"is a consequence of the grace of God"* (*HP*, p. 70). The ability to respond to the good news is not a natural human endowment; it is given through the experienced grace of the gospel. And while the specific expressions of the consequences explored in stage five may be quite varied, they are all based on the grace of "a *new situation* being created by the gospel—a new freedom to make choices we could never before make" (*HP*, p. 72).

The homiletical plot, according to Eugene Lowry, moves in sequence through the stages of upsetting the equilibrium, analyzing the discrepancy, disclosing the clue to resolution, experiencing the gospel, and anticipating the consequences. It is an "event-in-time" or, more accurately, an ordering of time which derives its shape and movement from the formal organization of narrative art. This sequential movement, moreover, is essential for effective proclamation of the gospel. As has been seen, dire homiletical consequences will predictably follow from a disregard of the plot; i.e., if the bind is not specifically portrayed and diagnosed, or if the clue to resolution leading to reversal is not appropriately disclosed. Some modifications of the stages in the plot can and should be made, however, as dictated by pastoral circumstances. A funeral sermon, for example, needs little if any attention to the first stage, for congregational equilibrium is already quite upset. And festival occasions may call for less time spent in diagnosis of the discrepancy. Moreover, "there come those extraordinary moments in the life of the church when a pastor faithful to the gospel and to conscience must bring a prophetic, healing, troubled, or celebrative witness to the congregation which by its very nature violates any and all sermonic rules" (*HP*, p. 78).

Apart from such special and infrequent occasions, the major exemption to the homiletical plot occurs when preaching from biblical narrative itself. The reasoning here is that such narrative material already has a plot of its own and therefore contains its own ambiguity to be resolved. "It does not need another plot line superimposed on top of it" (*HP*, p. 76). (The focus of *Doing Time in the Pulpit* seems more oriented toward this narration of a biblical story.) Such biblical narrative "should be allowed to run its own narrative course" (*HP*, p. 77). When the sermonic focus is elsewhere— life situational, doctrinal, or expository—the homiletical plot enables this preaching to become a "narrative event" as well. For Lowry, the purpose is, after all, that all preaching becomes an ordering of time into narrative time, the time of *our* story and *the* story.

Evaluation

Any evaluation of Eugene Lowry's homiletical method must begin by commending him for dealing so explicitly with method. Little effort is needed to pry his methodological considerations loose from the more general homiletical discussion. *The Homiletical Plot* and *Doing Time in the Pulpit* are veritable road maps of his approach to sermon preparation and delivery. If Charles Rice and Henry Mitchell encourage the preacher to "tell the story," Eugene Lowry adds his encouragement by offering the preacher two handbooks on narrative preaching. This should be appreciated.

Lowry's more basic analysis of the radical distinction between space-oriented discursive preaching and time-oriented narrative preaching is also quite helpful, and right on target. Sermonic trading in ideas, whatever organization they are given, is a static, lifeless, and reductionist enterprise. This ordering of ideas will need to give way to an ordering of experience with an attendant focus on eventfulness and happening. As well as anyone, Eugene Lowry has both portrayed the revolution in preaching and articulated the radical, systemic differences between ideational and narra-tive-based models. After reading Lowry, the preacher should be able to grasp quite clearly the alternative and antithetical approaches related to space and time.

Moreover, the employment of the insights of such literary critics as Crites, Kermode, and Roth as well as those of scholars who utilize these insights for biblical criticism (Amos Wilder, Norman Perrin, and Dan Otto Via, for example) considerably strengthens Lowry's presentation of a homileti-cal method based on a narrative paradigm. The analysis of the elements of narrative provided by Wesley Kort is especially helpful in the explication of narrative in *Doing Time in the Pulpit.* A narrative approach to homiletical method needs to be particularly attentive to the contributions of literary criticism at this point, and Lowry has listened well.

Any theological or homiletical method must be evaluated from the perspective of its internal consistency and formal congruence. In other words, the question must be asked whether Lowry has been both consistent in his use of the literary-critical sources as well as faithful to them in the development of his homiletical method. Several concerns emerge regarding this issue of methodological consistency:

1. By the references to a "sermonic idea" which informs the homiletical plot, Lowry appears to be retaining vestiges of an ideational approach while in general repudiating such a system. In fact, his references to the "theme" which is thrown against a problem as a plot is born suggest that the resultant plot can be reduced to an ideational ground. Such a suggestion is in strong contrast to his treatment of metaphor, since one of metaphor's most evocative qualities for preaching and theology is its fundamental resistance to ideational redaction.[11] Narrative artists themselves as well as literary critics of narrative seem to be quite clear at this point. A theme or topic is not essential to the control of narrative movement and meaning. Plot, as Lowry is aware, *is* the organizing principle, and such a principle does not depend necessarily on a thematic point of control. Such a view would seem to obtain not only for narrative art, but for the homiletical plot as well.

2. Although Lowry suggests that a sermonic plot based on biblical narrative should be allowed to "run its own narrative course," he does indicate a normative plotting of other sermonic approaches. This homiletical plot, with its five sequential stages, is presented as the formal expression of narrative art. That is, narrative plot is viewed as essentially constituted by these respective stages, which introduce ambiguity, sustain suspense, and resolve by way of reversal. Any sermon which lacks these constituent phases in sequence is viewed by Lowry as inadequate in its dealing with the particulars of the human situation and the gospel's response. But while this homiletician has made a strong case for the sermonic plot to be viewed as an "event-in-time," the specific warrants for "Lowry's loop" are not as evident. What seems to be at stake here is a hermeneutical bias toward a Hellenistic model of catharsis as the normative expression of narrative plot. Lowry, however, has already indicated that narrative plots in Scripture should be free from this sequence in order to "run their own course." If biblical narrative seems to offer any number of plot forms—including, but not restricted to, those of reversal—does it seem wise to have all non-narra-

tive-based sermons depend on the "loop" alone? Consequently, it must be concluded that this cathartic principle of plot structure is unnecessarily introduced from a position external to Lowry's own best analysis of narrative. Such usage of reversal may be quite appropriately applied to elements of Pauline dialectic or, certainly, to many of the parables. But the case is still far from being made that all non-narrative biblical pericopes relate easily to such a narrative sermonic shape.

3. The methodological discrepancy in Eugene Lowry's homiletic may be that he depicts the scope of appropriate sermonic form to include either narrative sermons informed by the plot of the specific biblical narrative or other sermons (life situational, doctrinal, etc.) expressed through a normative homiletical plot (the "loop"). From the perspective of a literary-critical interpretation of Scripture, however, alternatives to narrative include a wide range of other types of literature, each of which is organized according to its own internal logic. Why make a shift, then, from a sermonic form based on biblical form (as in narrative) to a sermonic form which overlooks the pericope's form while imposing an external one? Even if Lowry's five stages are granted to be absolutely essential expressions of narrative plot (which this writer does not accept) it does not follow that a narrative model should always be imposed on non-narrative biblical material. An alternative would be to analyze each specific biblical passage from the perspective of its own logic expressed through structure and movement. Such plotting would then certainly inform the sermonic plot, but would not be restricted to an assumed normative model of narrative form.

4. Finally, let us for a moment ignore the previous considerations and agree with Lowry on the essentiality of his homiletical plot. Taking his advice, we would spend a considerable portion of sermonic time and attention on analysis and diagnosis—occasionally devoting over half of the sermon to this task. Certainly, in-depth analysis of the specific human bind at stake is important, given his methodology.

But it is already a chronic failing of preachers and those who would learn to preach to devote excessive amounts of time to an analysis of human problems—i.e., sin, injustice, and illness are given much attention in pulpits already. The problem for the preacher is to learn to adequately, if not lavishly, image and proclaim grace, freedom, and gospel. "Experiencing the gospel" may then be the heart of the challenge surrounding the movement to renew preaching in the church. Lowry's strong reminder of this may be his best gift to us.

SWEPT UPSTREAM

Eugene Lowry

MARK 14:1-10 (RSV)

It was now two days before the Passover and the feast of Unleavened Bread. And the chief priests and the scribes were seeking how to arrest him by stealth, and kill him; for they said, "Not during the feast, lest there be a tumult of the people." And while he was at Bethany in the house of Simon the leper, as he sat at table, a woman came with an alabaster flask of ointment of pure nard, very costly, and she broke the flask and poured it over his head. But there were some who said to themselves indignantly, "Why was the ointment thus wasted? For this ointment might have been sold for more than three hundred denarii, and given to the poor." And they reproached her. But Jesus said, "Let her alone; why do you trouble her? She has done a beautiful thing to me. For you always have the poor with you, and whenever you will, you can do good to them; but you will not always have me. She has done what she could; she has anointed my body beforehand for burying. And truly, I say to you, wherever the gospel is preached in the whole world, what she has done will be told in memory of her."

Then Judas Iscariot, who was one of the twelve, went to the chief priests in order to betray him to them.

It is not your ordinary evening dinner party: good food, pleasant conversation, and an all around happy time. This is a pre-execution dinner of somber farewell!

While others are plotting on the outside, these folks on the inside are trying to survive the grief. Moments feel like days, with conversation—if you can call it that—composed mostly of denial by flat jokes, untimely reminiscences, and awkward silences. (Well, what *would* you say at a moment like that?) Even eye contact becomes almost unbearable.

They are doing the best they can—looking for every possible opportunity to show him their love—to express their appreciation without being obvious about it. But, of course, everything *is* obvious. It is going to be a very long evening. And then—all of a sudden—this woman bursts in!!

The text says nothing about her knocking politely and being

escorted to the dinner table. She simply comes in, uninvited, unannounced.

Jesus' friends are so shocked by this untimely behavior that nothing is said until she has already completed the deed of breaking the alabaster jar and pouring the ointment all over his head.

By this time the friends collect themselves enough to begin mumbling: "What a waste! Why, that ointment is outlandishly expensive—probably nine months' wages! And just think about the poor; think what could be done with all that money in behalf of the needy!"

The text says they "reproached her"—which translated likely means: "They let her have it!" Probably took turns, making sure the point of offense was quite clear. But Jesus hasn't had his turn yet.

All eyes turn toward him. "Won't take long for him to get it said—perhaps this is the occasion for a sermonette on priorities—a favorite theme. Something about seeking first the Kingdom, no doubt."

But he doesn't! He doesn't rebuke her! And they are shocked for the second time.

And we have to be shocked too, because their logic was quite in order: Nine months' salary for one brief moment of dramatic show—when human need lies all around?!

But by the time we can begin to ask just why he didn't see the logic of their complaint, we hear Jesus' reply. He gives a rebuke all right—aimed not at her, but at them—his hosts for the evening: "Leave her alone!" he demands, and begins to speak about the unspeakable—about his imminent execution—why, "She has anointed my body beforehand for burying!" My God, he's said it! The horrible, the awful, the unbearable truth!

And that comment about her having "done what she could"—what's that supposed to mean? They had been doing the best they could all evening. Was that not good enough?

Or was Jesus questioning the motives behind their objection? Was he implying that he was uncertain whether their reaction to her grew out of *her* lack of an invitation or *their* abundance of dignity? Were they presuming that their show of affection was deserving while hers was undeserving?

Frankly, the whole scene is confused, and we reel back and forth, agreeing with one side, then another:

Why doesn't Jesus understand the logic of their objection?
Why don't they understand the nature of her gesture?
Why doesn't he see the waste?
Why don't they see the Grace?
Why?   Why?

Obviously we have a bit of a communication problem here. Jesus and his dinner friends seem on utterly different wavelengths—(the kindest way I know to put it). Indeed, we've got apples and oranges here!

In order to unravel the problem, we turn to the philosophy of Jean Kerr in her exposition on the human condition, in *Please Don't Eat the Daisies.* She says: "If you can keep your head about you when all others around you are losing theirs, it's just quite possible that you don't get the picture."

They just didn't get the picture! That's all—they missed the magnificent moment of celebration.

Celebration, after all, has a mind of its own, a different logic altogether, and demands an utterly different set of behaviors. Apples and oranges. Like the point of a joke, either you get it or you don't. Well, they didn't get it.

I don't know whether Jesus' friends were so conservative that their piety would not allow them to turn loose into celebration, or whether they were so liberal they had lost any reason for celebration. Whichever or whatever, they managed to apply ordinary logic to an extraordinary event. Never works.

I remember being dropped off at a motel one Saturday afternoon in Carbondale, Illinois, prior to a weekend preaching. I turned on the TV set just in time to see some college team score a touchdown. I sensed something strange about the crowd reaction—or its lack of reaction. Soon the same team scored again. Ho-hum—and then I learned that these were touchdowns number 3 and 4 of an already boring game. I believe the final score was Nebraska 34; UCLA 3. Not much reason for celebration—not any more. Victory had become certain.

Later that very same afternoon, I turned to the final few minutes of another game—between Georgia and somebody—and I thought the hometown fans were going to tear the concrete stadium down to the ground—as the underdogs pulled a surprising upset in the final moments of play. Celebration! The impossible had just happened. And that's the key to understanding celebration—hers or anyone else's! Celebration occurs *only* when the impossible happens. There's never much hoopla over the expected—but the unexpected may turn us loose.

You know how it goes: You're clicking your heels in absolute glee for having accomplished what could not be done. What was it—the term paper in on time, the impossible sale, the meal ready for the unexpected guests—whatever! But unbelievably, it happened, it got done. Up comes your logical friend who has no use for such nonsense: "What do you mean, it was impossible? You did it didn't you? Obviously you simply miscalculated the thing."

About all you can say is: "If you can't join the celebration, leave me alone!"—which is exactly what Jesus said to the uncelebrative set of friends: "Leave her alone!" Otherwise put: "Don't knock what you don't understand!"

True enough, we don't know *what* it was that turned her loose that day, but we do know *why!* There *had* to have been some previous, powerful encounter with Jesus—which somehow turned everything around, making the impossible possible. And whenever that happens: logical decorum and proper dignity, get out of the way; here comes the ointment!

And, we don't even know who she was:

Was she Mary Magdalene, whose previous life-style was replaced with new hope born of forgiveness?

Was she a member of an oppressed group, and Jesus had convinced her she was somebody, that God don't make no trash?

Well, we don't have a name nor the particulars—but *we do know* that somehow, somewhere:

She had been at the end of her rope and Jesus offered her more;

92

She had been up against the wall and Jesus moved the wall;
She was utterly without hope—until Jesus came along with new life.

Unbelievable! Impossible!

And true . . . It was time to celebrate!

No wonder Jesus (who apparently knew the details of her joy) said, "What she has done is a beautiful thing!"

And then he said something that so far as we know, he never said any other time or about any other person. He said: "Wherever the gospel is preached in all the world, what she has done will be told in memory of her." Magnificent!

But wait, "In memory of *her*"? Who is dying, anyway? Why didn't he say: "Wherever the gospel is preached in all the world, what she has done will be told as a memorial to me?" In memory of *her*? After all, he is the one about to be betrayed with a kiss and be hung on a cross!

Yet, as she rushes up in glorious, grateful joy—and anoints his head with oil, *he knows* it must represent her entire life savings—spent now in the ecstasy of celebration! Of course he knows it is a memorial to him, but its magnificence now becomes a tribute to her as well. *She couldn't give more—and would not give less!*

A woman—swept upstream with gratitude.
Sad friends of Jesus—ever so self-consciously prepared to commemorate his impending death.
And Jesus—Jesus, although facing certain death, yet unself-consciously prepared to celebrate *her* impending life.

And that made all the difference in the world that night. *And it still does.*

NOTES

1. Eugene L. Lowry, *The Homiletical Plot: The Sermon as Narrative Art Form* (Atlanta: John Knox Press, 1980), p. 12. (Hereafter *HP*.)

2. W. E. Sangster, *The Craft of Sermon Construction* (Philadelphia: Westminster Press, 1951).

3. J. Randall Nichols, *Building the Word: The Dynamics of Communication and Preaching* (San Francisco: Harper & Row, 1980).

4. Eugene L. Lowry, *Doing Time in the Pulpit: The Relationship Between Narrative and Preaching* (Nashville: Abingdon Press, 1985), pp. 14-26. (Hereafter *DT*.)

5. *DT*, p. 23. See pp. 18 ff. for Lowry's explication of plot.

6. The term "method of distillation" is developed by David Buttrick. See chapter 5.

7. Barbara Hardy, quoted in *DT*, p. 39.

8. Wesley Kort, *Narrative Elements and Religious Meaning* (Philadelphia: Fortress Press, 1975).

9. Ibid., p. 40.

10. Ibid., p. 41.

11. See Robert W. Funk, *Language, Hermeneutic, and Word of God* (New York: Harper & Row, 1966), pp. 152 ff.

4

FRED CRADDOCK

The Inductive Method in Preaching

The nemesis of preaching, according to Fred Craddock, is a deductive methodology which has held sway for centuries, having its origins in Aristotle. This method derives its name from an internal movement and logic; beginning with a general truth, its goal is to lead to specific applications for a particular situation. "Simply stated, deductive movement is from the general truth to the particular application or experience."[1] Within homiletical tradition, this deductive method has long been established as normative for preaching regarding both the structure of a sermon and its exegetical underpinnings. Structurally, a recognizable form is consistently detected: the thesis of the sermon is stated and broken down into its constitutive "points"; and these subtheses are then expanded, illustrated, and finally applied to some particular life situation. This approach is immediately familiar, expressing "the main stream of traditional preaching" (*AOW*, p. 54).

If the formal characteristics of this mainstream approach to preaching are familiar, so are its uses of Scripture. Deductive preaching has exemplified a minimalist and often arbitrary relationship to biblical material throughout its history. The thesis or topic may or may not be drawn from the Bible, biblical warrant and authority being by no means essential to the deductive method. Scripture can usually be found within the range of illustrative material, or may

Fred Craddock is professor of New Testament and homiletics, Candler School of Theology, Emory University, Atlanta, Georgia.

contribute "a governing image or basic vocabulary."[2]
Deductive preaching's use of Scripture, however, most often
constitutes genuine misuse. Passages evaluated for employment within the deductive preaching model are first boiled
down, revealing a thematic residue. Otherwise, serving as
illustrations, biblical texts are viewed as merely ornaments to
the argument already presented. Such use, according to
Craddock, only offers "the illusion rather than the reality of
listening to the text" (*Preaching*, p. 100).

Beyond deductive preaching's exegetical deficiencies, two
other serious problems have flawed this mainstream tradition. Craddock notes that the thesis of the sermon first is
expounded and only later is related to particular situations.
He then adds that such an approach is "a most unnatural
mode of communication, unless, of course, one presupposes
passive listeners who accept the right or authority of the
speaker to state conclusions which he then applies to their
faith and life" (*AOW*, p. 54). There is, therefore, an inherent
bias in the whole project of deductive preaching which
assumes authoritarian address of God's Word and passive
reception (*AOW*, p. 54). What is lacking in such a downward
movement of truth is any possibility of dialog or democracy.
There is "no listening by the speaker, no contributing by the
hearer. . . . If the congregation is on the team, it is as javelin
catcher" (*AOW*, p. 56). Such an attitude is seriously out of
touch with contemporary American congregations, Craddock believes. Some other, less autocratic method of
preaching should replace the deductive sermon's condescending manner.

A second major flaw in deductive preaching relates to issues
of structure and movement. As the main thesis is broken down
into subsidiary points, a structure emerges which presents
almost insurmountable problems regarding homiletic movement. The hearers of a traditional three-point sermon
frequently experience three sermonettes instead, since the
transition from the end of one point to the beginning of the
next is usually unsuccessful. "There may have been some
movement within each point," Craddock observes, "and there

may have been some general kinship among the points, but there was not one movement from beginning to end" (*AOW*, p. 56). Points that are conceptually equal in force cannot evoke a sense of sermonic movement and unity. Attempts at communication through such a static system are experienced by people in the church today as unnatural and as a violation of a sense of community (*AOW*, p. 56).

The increasingly problematic status of traditional preaching is due both to its inherent methodological liabilities and to a general deterioration in its relationship both to church and to culture. Most noticeably, a crisis in language has been experienced generally as a loss of the power of words. There has been a diminution in the ability of words to express potency: "to create or to destroy, to bind or to loose, to bless or to curse" (*AOW*, p. 5). If such a crisis in language has afflicted the more general cultural dimensions of speech, then a crisis in preaching must result as well. It is important, therefore, that the one who would preach understand the causes of this strange loss of the power of words. Professor Craddock suggests several contributing factors. First, he notes that people daily are bombarded by words received primarily through the media. "The eyes and ears have no relief, and all the old silent haunts are now scarred with billboards and invaded by public-address systems" (*AOW*, pp. 6-7). Without silence, the power of words decays, both in social and ecclesial contexts. Biblically speaking, the Word of God is born in silence, and when silence is lost, words and the Word seem to lose their potency.[3] "How one understands a word as an event in the world of sound depends to a great extent upon whether that word is experienced against a backdrop of silence or in a room of many words" (*Preaching*, p. 52). Most of us are living in rooms of many words.

Craddock locates a second reason for loss of efficacy in the traditional language of the church. Although a crisis of culture-wide proportions, the language of the church seems most susceptible to the disease. On one level, this may relate to the inability of the church to slough old and worn-out words which functioned effecively at one time but which no longer communicate the faith. These words "fought well at Nicea, Chalcedon and Augsburg," but "they are kept in the line of march even if the whole mission is slowed to a snail's pace and observers on the side are bent double with laughter" (*AOW*, p. 7).

The crisis in religious language is far more extensive than this inability to let go of anachronistic terminology. Our whole culture has been significantly affected by a scientific paradigm of truth and meaning. Words have become understood "as signs, as indicators pointing to information that can be verified" (*AOW*, pp. 7-8). A church which capitulates to such a "sterilizing reductionism" would thereby lose the evocative and performative sense of the power of its linguistic tradition. Myth and metaphor would come under suspicion and even the term "God" would become problematic. In fact, Craddock maintains, we are watching this come to pass.[4]

A final factor which has had an impact upon the power of words is the advent of television and its visually oriented "world." Even though preaching stands solidly within a tradition of oral communication whose lineage is rooted in Scripture itself, the modern culture may now be favoring the eye over the ear. If human receptivity "is no longer polarized around sound and person but rather around sight and object, the difficulties for the preaching task are all too obvious" (*AOW*, p. 9). These difficulties for preaching can also be traced to a prior shift in language's center of gravity. With the advent of a print-oriented culture, oral communication was viewed as subsidiary to the written word, radically changing previous experience of Scripture. "Words fixed in space by print tended to create the idea that the meanings of these words were fixed also. As a result, the written word was more authoritative than the spoken" (*AOW*, p. 10). The more recent shift from a literary to a visually oriented culture really represents a second profound shift in social consciousness away from the primacy of oral communication. The situation is not this neat in its cultural and linguistic orientations, however, and this is a sign of hope for Craddock. The

renewal of preaching may be assisted by renewed appreciation for the power of language in oral address.

Beyond the crucial dimensions of the crisis in language,
other cultural factors have also contributed to the problematic state of preaching in the churches. The traditional
perspective which saw reality as substance within a static
modality has given way to philosophical positions emphasiz-
ing being and time. Metaphysics has been displaced by
ontology and historicity. The culture reflects this disintegra-
tion of the old substantial universe in its art, its architecture,
and its music. The ordered and changeless qualities of a
previous era are gone, replaced by art which expresses rapid
change and fragmentation. Architecturally, even churches
"do not look like churches any more!" (*AOW*, pp. 12-13)
Within such a worship space, the static and timeless verities
contained within a three-point sermon seem oddly out of
place and out of touch. The hearers of such preaching
receive it as the imposition of a false symmetry on life, caught
up in rapid and discordant change.

In spite of all this shaking of the cultural foundations,
Craddock notes, "the sermons of our time have, with few
exceptions, kept the same form" (*AOW*, p. 13). The message
is clear to those who listen for the gospel—the sermon reflects
a different world than the one they live in. In that sermon
world truths come self-evident and prepackaged and a sense
of temporality is missing. Yet the mainstream orthodoxy of
deductive preaching persists, posing for many preachers a
serious dilemma. Either the sermon conforms to all the
criteria of a proper sermon—points, outlines, illustrations,
and all—or it becomes a kind of second class offering of
subjective thoughts and feelings. In either case, the preacher
feels ill at ease and somewhat compromised and asks whether
he or she "should continue to serve up a monologue in a
dialogical world" (*AOW*, p. 16).

Of course, there is another side to these questions; the
whole project of preaching in the church has never been easy.
It perennially involves both intense private reflection and
public ministry; a capability to use words yet a dependence on

99

the Word beyond words; and the courage to address the listener with the Word as well as the storyteller's skills in sharing the biblical Story. Given these demands and expectations, one readily is able to agree with Craddock when he observes that preaching itself is a very complex activity (*Preaching*, p. 16). Moreover, the church's loss of some of its potential preachers in the face of these challenges may be a poignant testimony to the power of preaching: "it is demanding, exhausting, painful, and for all involved, creates a crisis, a moment of truth, a decision situation of immense consequence" (*AOW*, p. 17). This call for decision which is at the heart of the ministry of preaching lays a claim on both the speaker and the listener, and the continuing response of ministers and seminarians is perhaps the best testimony to the resilience of this ministry.

> There are also other signs of hope, ironically involving some of the same key fields of concern which have been perceived as contributing to preaching's crisis. Fred Craddock revisits the study of language and discovers a major source of encouragement for those who find the pulpit a "dry and waterless place." On the one hand, linguistic analysis has its positivistic expression, calling into question religious language's use of symbol, myth, and metaphor. But on the other hand, a more recent, lively interest in "primitivism" has led to "a general acceptance of the priority of words or speaking in the constitution and expression of reality" (*AOW*, p. 34). Craddock rehearses some of the central contributions of Martin Heidegger at this point concerning the cruciality of language. Language precedes human existence and gives rise to it. Viewed from this perspective, language is constitutive of human existence and is essential to it. A person "is a conversation" (*AOW*, p. 37). And since preaching is by its very nature born out of an oral tradition and becomes an event by returning the Word to its oral/aural immediacy, the performative power of its language is now reaffirmed. Recalling the insights of Carl Michalson, Craddock concludes that "preaching is by its nature an acoustical event, having its home in orality not textuality" (*Preaching*, p. 31).

Another encouragement related to this deeper appreciation of language sharpens the distinction between written and spoken words. The former are given, fixed, and available all at once for scrutiny. The latter, however, are never all present to the listener, yet the spoken word is only given in the present. Hence, "sound is always present, always an existential experience" (*AOW*, p. 29). Moreover, the spoken word in a non-rehearsed situation, such as preaching, conveys qualities of openness, polyvalence, and spontaneity. More is given in such oral/aural circumstances than initially intended. Moreover, the immediacy of spoken communication tends toward a future fulfillment. The "more than was intended" opens up a new future, the spoken word can lead "toward a goal yet undetermined" (*AOW*, p. 29). Finally, by virtue of the primacy of the spoken word, an inherently corporate dimension of God's revelatory activity is disclosed. Never occurring in isolation, the spoken word is both a sign and a cause of life together. "It presupposes that which it also creates: community" (*AOW*, p. 43).

Preeminent among the hopeful signs for a renewal of the pulpit is the state of the relationship between biblical studies and proclamation. The two disciplines, Craddock observes, are discovering a relationship of mutuality and interdependence which have not been too evident in their recent history. But now, proclamation and biblical studies find that the former can give the latter "its reason and motive," while conversely, "biblical scholarship can keep proclamation athletically trim, free of superstition and sloppy sentimentality."[5] Proclamation and biblical studies are linked in another, more profound sense as well. Any attempt to clarify the task of preaching leads necessarily to a study of the biblical text; upon further study that text is unveiled as an aspect of the preaching of the New Testament church.[6] One of the most important insights of biblical scholarship, therefore, is the disclosure of the relationship between Scripture and the preaching of the early church.

On the other hand, the dominant tenor of the relationship between biblical studies and preaching has been somewhat negative and abrasive. The emergence of the historical-critical study of Scripture had as one of its objectives the understandability of the Bible by the church. Ironically, the reverse has become the norm. What was conveyed to the church, and especially to the preacher, by the probings of historical criticism was an increasing awareness of the differences between the contemporary world and the biblical world. As it was dissected by historical research, the text seemed to recede further and further, as if viewed through the wrong end of a telescope. An experience of distance was the outcome: the preacher felt a disturbing distance from the biblical world and a confusing distance from the scholarly one. Faced with this quandary, some preachers reverted to pre-seminary methods of dealing with a text and simply ignored the critical apparatus a seminary education had sought to impart. More to the point was the insight that "biblical studies always moved [the preacher] backward, behind the texts to sources and antecedents, while [the preacher] at the same time sensed that in actuality, the story of the Gospel had always moved forward" (*RNT*, p. 77). What was needed was "a new angle of vision" within biblical interpretation which would allow the preacher to traverse this distance between him or herself and the world of the biblical text.[7]

It is of crucial significance for preaching that "the distance between the modern pulpit and the ancient text, a distance of which historical-critical methods made us so aware, no longer seems so frightening and non-negotiable" (*SUS*, p. 8). New methods of biblical interpretation have arisen within the last twenty-five years which are capable of offering this new angle of vision. Particularly in the rhetorical and literary criticism of Amos Wilder, Robert Funk, and Ernst Fuchs, the "inseparable relation of the Gospel and the forms of its communication" has been established" (*AOW*, p. 45). Faced with such a multiplicity of literary forms in Scripture—narrative, sayings, hymns, epistolary discourse, and so on—the preacher may finally be convinced to let go of the constraints of the old topical outline and its points and poems. Whatever sermonic method is chosen, its "mode of discourse" will be appropriate to the form of the pericope itself (*AOW*, p. 45). Just as there is no one normative form of biblical discourse, a biblical sermon will not impose any particular sermonic form, especially one derived from Hellenistic rhetoric, upon every text. While not supplanting the historical-critical approach, an invaluable contribution of literary criticism is its capability of helping the preacher to understand what a biblical text *does* as well as learning what it *says* (*SUS*, p. 8).

Prior to explicating the implications of this new angle of vision for homiletical method, one other contribution of the new biblical studies must be discussed because of its significance for and understanding of preaching. In spite of the distance between biblical text and contemporary situation, there is a continuum between the two ends of the hermeneutical arch which is essential for preaching. Biblical texts not only are discovered to have a past (form and redaction criticism) but a future as well. Theologically, this futurity of the text which is fulfilled in preaching is based for Craddock on several fundamental assumptions. The Scriptures:

[1] . . . are normative in the life of the church. To sever preaching from that norm either by neglect or intent would be to cut the church off from its primary source of nourishment and discipline. Sermons not informed and inspired by Scripture are objects dislodged, orphans in the world, without mother or father.

[2] . . . by keeping sentinel watch over the life and faith of the church, [blow] the whistle on lengthy exercises in self-analysis and self-saving. . . . Sermons that are self-serving are called into question by the very texts which had been selected to authenticate the message.

[3] . . . continually remind pulpit and pew not only what but how to preach. . . . A stirring text well read creates an expectation in listeners which the sermon should not disappoint (*Preaching*, p. 27).

If that expectation is to be fulfilled in the hearing of the congregation, it will not be through the imposition of a condescending, deductive method. Fred Craddock now leads the reader through a deeper consideration of the implications of the new biblical studies for a method of biblical preaching.

There is tension in the distance between preacher and text which must remain throughout the process of interpretation. Attempts at overcoming the distance, through, for instance, existentialism (which dissolves it) or positivism (which simply remains in the past and thus avoids interpretation), are for Craddock unacceptable alternatives. The distance remains, though the task of interpretation changes the quality of that distance, a shift which will be decisive for preaching. At the beginning of interpretation, however, the preacher will need to approach the ancient text "*anticipating* meaning"; that is, come to it with interest and expectation (*RNT,* p. 78). The preacher, then, "can come with *interest* knowing that interest is an accepted hermeneutical principle" (*RNT,* p. 78). Moreover, this interest should not be narrowly circumscribed by specifically homiletical concerns: "What is this text's message?" To shut down the interpretive process in such a fashion is to deny of Scripture its polyvalent character. A text contains a "surplus of meaning," even beyond that which was intended by the writer (*Preaching,* p. 115). No single interpretation will exhaust the meaning latent in a text for interpretation or for preaching. Anticipating the text's surplus of meaning, then, is a principle which stands at the outset of the preacher's challenge of negotiating the distance between Scripture and the contemporary situation.

The tendency of historical-critical analysis to increase a sense of distance between interpreter and text has already been explored. For Craddock, though, this distancing is especially problematic for the preacher, since he or she necessarily assumes that the present will be illumined by the passage of scripture and a sermon which deals with integrity with the lesson. Yet the two tasks, interpretation and preaching, do seem to be at cross purposes here. Within biblical studies, "the historical disciplines have looked upon the text as the *result* of certain events and interactions, while the preacher looks upon the text as the *cause,* the generator, of events and interactions" (*Preaching,* p. 113). At this stage of interpretation, with the initial application of historical-critical skills, the exegete-preacher receives the distinct impression that the text is "moving away from rather than toward the pulpit" (*Preaching*, p. 113). Fortunately there are major points of contact between text and interpreter which can serve, along with a constant interest and expectation, to reverse the sense of distancing and bring the text near. Craddock suggests five favorable factors which serve to establish points of contact between preacher and text.

A. "First, the distance between ourselves and the original readers of the text is in a measure bridged by our common humanity" (*Preaching*, p. 134). In many cases, the interpreter can quite easily recognize the commonality in the biblical and contemporary situations once issues of setting and cultural trappings have been addressed. What is required then is not thinking and feeling as would a first-century person, but simply as would any person.

B. "The second favorable factor is the continuity of the church and its tradition of interpreting the text" (*Preaching*, p. 135). Craddock observes here the historic and ecclesial nature of scriptural interpretation. The preacher today continues the apostolic succession of interpretation, based on two thousand years of how tradition handled the text.

C. "The third favorable factor . . . is the existence within the church of the community of scholars whose service to the church is to preserve the text as it has been received and to aid the church in understanding the text" (*Preaching*, p. 135). Simply put, the church needs the academy for the vital tasks related to the understanding of its Scripture. Although this relationship between community of faith and community of scholars has often been marked by tension, its intent and its fruit have been positive for all parties concerned.

D. "The fourth factor enabling interpretation is the presence of the Holy Spirit in the church" (*Preaching*, p. 135). It is not only through apostolic succession that the presence of the Word has been maintained through the course of the church's life. This promised Counselor is given that the church might remain in the truth. The work of the Spirit's inspiration was not delimited to the writing of the words of Scripture on the page, "but also . . . [to] getting them *off* again" (*RNT*, p. 78).

E. "The fifth and final factor contributing to interpretation as a vital and fruitful endeavor is the text itself" (*Preaching*, p. 136). Here, Craddock echoes the admonitions of those engaged in the new hermeneutic. It is not so much that the interpreter only asks questions of the text; in the process he or she is called into question by the text. The Scriptures exert a claim on the interpreter, which in and of itself is good news. Our self-understanding is changed when encountered by this surplus of meaning within the text.

These encouraging factors will not mean a complete resolution of the tension latent in the distance between text and interpreter. Rather, they are provided as a hermeneutical foundation for the task of interpretation, and as an encouragement to the interpreter that his or her efforts in this respect are significant and can obtain fulfillment in a biblical sermon.

All scriptural interpretation begins with the selection of a text, although sermons themselves may be prompted by occasions as well as texts and still remain biblical preaching.[8] The text may be chosen by the preacher (Craddock encourages the utilization of some sort of preaching plan) or commended by way of the lectionary. In any case, the initial question becomes, How is the preacher to approach the text? (*AOW*, p. 134) How is the "conversation" between the text and the listener to be initiated? Craddock indicates a three-stage process of interaction.

The first and perhaps most important aspect of interpretation is a sensitive but unassisted listening to the text. This is not the time for consulting secondary sources concerning the Scripture lesson—those investigations will come later. First, the text should be read, several times in fact, and the preacher should respond immediately with "ideas, questions, feelings, and triggered recollections."[9]

Such preliminary readings should have a quality of naivete about them, and the thoughts and feelings that constitute the interpreter's first response should be as spontaneous as possible. However, because of the spontaneity of this interaction, the responses are fragile and so it is best to write down everything that comes to mind.[10] Through such a discipline of naive reading and listening, the preacher is more closely identifying with the congregation "who will also come to the text unaided except for their own thoughts, feelings, and needs" (*Preaching*, p. 106). For this first reading, the preacher should find her or himself among the parishioners rather than among the scholars. Questions raised and recorded here will be most likely derived from the concerns of the text itself. One important reason for recording these reactions and responses, for Craddock, is that "these early notes will provide more than half of one's introductions to sermons" (*Preaching*, p. 106). For this purpose and several others as well, this naive first reading and rereading of the text is essential, "foundational for all other study."[11]

2 The second stage in the interpretive process involves the contributions of commentaries and other resources. The timing of this stage is crucial, though, since to consult a commentary too early may result in a weakening of the centrality of the text. Consulted too late, a commentary's influence is diminished and simply becomes another potential source for sermonic material. Craddock underlines this assertion: "A commentary consulted too soon tends to be a master over the interpreter and consulted too late tends to be an agreeable subordinate. At the right time, a commentary can be the interpreter's colleague."[12] Among the significant purposes of this second stage, an early activity involves "establishing the text." Variants in the text are checked along with its parameters, even if they are already indicated by the lectionary. "Taking the text seriously" Craddock notes, "begins by asking, What words did the writer write?"[13] Later in this second stage, the interpreter will seek the assistance of the commentaries in answering questions related to the meaning of the text in its original context. As clearly as possible, the preacher will want to discover how original

listeners understood the text when they heard it. Finally, the more specific issues raised as early as the first reading are investigated and given some resolution, if possible. The movement within this stage, then, is from more general concerns to the more specific and concrete.

The third and final stage of this particular process involves a movement away from the secondary sources and toward the text once more. Now, it is carefully reread and the notes made during the first reading are reviewed. What has happened, the preacher may observe, is that "the intervening exegetical work has clarified some early questions, confirmed some impressions, and destroyed others."[14] By this latter reading much of the initial distance in the text has disappeared and a deep engagement is taking its place. "If this is indeed the case," Craddock states, "then the process of withdrawing from the text and recovering one's distance from it should begin" (*Preaching*, p. 117). This new step of withdrawal is characterized by a more analytic relationship to the text which involves the following considerations:

1. "Position" in the text. The preacher is now called to become self-conscious about the "point of identification" or "position" in relation to the text. Redactional questions concerning the levels of the text are raised now and will soon become important for the development of the sermon. (For example, will the sermon focus on the parable alone or the evangelist's redactional context as well?) But to raise the question of position in the text is also to insist that the interpreter become aware of the place in the text he or she has already assumed. Where has the preacher stood within the narrative? With what character or characters? Is it not time for other perspectives to be taken? An intentionality about these considerations is important for two reasons, Craddock believes. In the first place, such identification will bear "not only upon the interpretation of the text but also upon the sermon soon to be designed" (*Preaching*, p. 118). In the second place, a lack of self-consciousness at this point will almost certainly assure that in both interpretation and preaching, the preacher will take the most favored places in the text. Given this temptation, it is certainly most healthy "to stand elsewhere now and then" (*AOW*, p. 139).

2. *Discerning the theme*. A major achievement in interpretation is the ability to state in one affirmative sentence the theme or message of the text. The affirmative mode of this theme sentence serves to avoid "the hortatory terms that too often characterize entire sermons: we must, we ought, we should, let us, let us not" (*Preaching*, p. 122). Craddock does not mean to say that such exhortation is out of place in preaching; rather, this step is intended to relate such imperatives functionally to the theme. The ability to capture the meaning of the text in one sentence, he affirms, "marks a genuine achievement, rewarded not only by a sense of satisfaction but by a new appetite for the next task: the sermon itself" (*Preaching*, p. 122).

3. *Discerning the action*. A text not only says something (its theme), but does something as well. Actions along with words constitute the fullness of human communication. With reference to Scripture, this activity of the text is best discerned by attention to its historical and literary contexts and to its form (*Preaching*, p. 123). For Fred Craddock, what a text does reveals its intentionality—e.g., does a passage of scripture reprove, encourage, mistrust, correct? An awareness of the scripture's context, of course, is vital for such obtaining discernment.

Discovering what a text does, moreover, is intimately related to sermon preparation, especially if the sermon is intended to do what the text does. The preacher, then, "will want to hold onto the form, since form captures and conveys function, not only during the interpretation of the text but during the designing of the sermon as well" (*Preaching*, p. 123). The difficulty with a thematic-deductive approach to the sermon would be that this principle is consistently violated. The form of the text is abandoned for a deductive model presumed to be normative apart from the form and function of the text. It is little wonder, Craddock notes, that such literary forms as the parables of Jesus suffered homiletical violence through such a thematic approach.

These canons for biblical interpretation, Fred Craddock believes, will provide the preacher/interpreter with a broad understanding of the text, its message, its context, and its literary form. However, while quite a bit may now be known about the scripture, little may be known about the sermon itself. This awareness is critical for preaching: "the process of arriving at something to say is to be distinguished from the process of determining how to say it" (*Preaching,* p. 84). For Craddock, a distinction of interpretive method from homiletical method, strictly speaking, is based on several key assumptions. First, it is assumed that work on the sermon itself is necessary subsequent to the exegetical and interpretive tasks which will provide the sermon's message. Until that message has been determined, "getting up a sermon" is a fruitless and potentially chaotic activity. On the other hand, the achievement of a text's theme and form does not necessarily provide the preacher with the shape and context of the sermon. Each process, interpretation and sermon design, is distinct, having its own goals, skills, and climax (*Preaching,* p. 85). Moreover, each process has its own critical focus or position, with a distance between them which gives rise to the hermeneutical task. While "factors of time, space, language, world view, and immediate circumstances" separate the two, the distance may be negotiated. However, the two enterprises are simply not susceptible to one encompassing methodology.

The shift from arriving at a message to determining how that message will be preached occurs as the preacher turns to the task of interpreting the listeners. Not only must the preacher interpret the Scriptures with understanding, but he or she must interpret the congregation as well. Otherwise, the sermon will remain in the past or the message will be presented in an overly objective manner, removed from the concerns of the hearers. When undertaking this second project of interpretation, though, the same question of distance which was so crucial to biblical interpretation also stands with regard to the hearers. For Craddock, it is best to begin the process of the interpretation of the listeners at a considerable distance; the congregation should first be viewed by the preacher as an audience. This at least removes the temptation to gear the sermon from the start according to the likes and dislikes of specific members of the congregation. Viewed positively, however, the goal here is "to get enough distance to understand and accept the listeners in and of themselves, apart from their relationship to the minister" (*Preaching*, p. 87). The purpose of this act of the imagination is to remind the preacher of the needs and values held in common by a congregation, apart from those brought to the foreground by pastoral involvements. Here, the challenge is to see the congregation as a guest minister would see them—as those created in the image of God, yet an image distorted by sin and rebellion. There is, still, "the faint recollection of Eden" within any such group of listeners, which will evoke a sense of recognition when the preacher speaks of the Christian faith and the human condition (*Preaching*, p. 88). Other qualities of listeners seen as audience will also begin to gain definition. "They are all seeking a place to stand, a place that feels like home"; they want "room to say no to the sermon but a genuine invitation to say yes" (*Preaching*, pp. 88-89). Finally, the listeners understood as audience have a longing to be brought into God's presence. Any sermon which addresses these needs will have significantly overcome the distance between pulpit and pew. Even those hearers who are not church members will feel that the minister has understood them well (*Preaching*, p. 90).

Although the listeners as audience are viewed as strangers, this sense of distance is diminished when the listeners are seen as a congregation. Now, the specific characteristics of the persons and groups within the church are taken into account. What is also considered is the powerful relationship that exists between pastor and congregation. Put together, the knowledge accumulated through this process will enable the pastor "to preach with a power and effectiveness unavailable to the guest speaker, whatever may be the skills, credentials, and reputation of that speaker" (*Preaching*, p. 91). Whether by way of formal means (initial pastoral contact with community officials), informal means (the daily pastoral contacts), or by way of "empathetic imagination" (putting oneself in the place of parishioners), such an understanding of listeners as congregation is indispensable to effective preaching. Yet Craddock notes that this more intimate and specific awareness does not displace the understanding gained by viewing the hearers as audience. On the contrary, the concrete details gained through pastoral ministry and empathetic imagination build on the foundation gained from viewing the listeners from a greater distance. By employing both approaches, "ministers will likely be surprised to discover how much understanding of the human condition they already have but which has not been adequately reflected in either the words or music of their preaching" (*Preaching,* p. 97).

There is a need, Craddock argues, for both critical distance from and close identification with a preacher's congregation. The former provides for an essential clarity of identity with respect to both preacher and people. Without such a sense of appropriate distance, identification can become too intense and can become emotionally consuming (*Preaching,* p. 40). Yet preaching without an identification with the listeners loses the ability to move, to convict, and to even communicate the biblical message. Moreover, such undue distance misses the important point that preaching is inherently dialogical; the people are participants in the sermon along with the preacher. An initial caution based upon this participation is that one's preaching "does not put down, insult, violate, or ignore those whose investment in the message is no less than that of the speaker" (*Preaching,* p. 25). Assessed constructively, Fred Craddock offers three points for consideration relative to the importance of a sense of identification. First, there is a need for the sermon to be appropriate to the hearers if they are to become participants in the dialog. Actually, Craddock insists, the congregation's participation in the sermon precedes its birth. "The listeners speak to the preacher before the preacher speaks to them; the minister listens before saying anything" (*Preaching,* p. 25). Sermons are not general addresses to an anonymous audience, but a specific message at a certain time to real people in a concrete situation. Preaching must be appropriate to that context. Second, Craddock urges that the very design of the sermon invite maximum participation of the congregation: "sermons should proceed or move in such a way as to give the listener something to think, feel, decide, and do during the preaching" (*Preaching*, p. 25). Finally, Craddock argues that the value of participation means that the sermon "should speak *for* as well as *to* the congregation" (*Preaching*, p. 26). He does not mean to convey permission for the preacher to simply serve up a diet of things a congregation wants to hear. Rather, what is meant is that the preacher should occasionally be willing to articulate in his or her preaching what the people want to say. Such a sermon would have *God* as the primary audience and *evoke* from the people a realization that their words to God have been said from the pulpit.

If the sermon speaks for the people as well as to them, then there is much more likelihood that recognition will occur. That is, the congregation would be allowed to recover what was experienced in the past and to sense it as being familiar. "It is part of the power of preaching," Craddock affirms, "that the people are familiar with what we are saying."[15] Effective preaching evokes these past experiences and a corresponding sense of familiarity, creating what Craddock terms a "nod of recognition." In other words, the power of preaching is not located in its constant novelty, but in its ability to bring to recognition what people already know, allowing them to say, "Amen." With regard to sermon preparation, Craddock underscores two values which need to be inherent if a nod of recognition is to occur. "First, it means that the preacher will share, not omit, details" (*Preaching*, p. 161). People need to be entrusted with the biblical story, but recognition will occur only if enough detail is present for that story to be recalled. Second, the nod of recognition is evoked when the preacher recounts the familiar with interest and enthusiasm. Craddock notes that some preachers deal ponderously with biblical material because the people have heard it before. What these preachers are failing to grasp is the excitement which is created when people recognize their stories, and thereby recognize themselves in the message. "The principle of recognition liberates the preacher to move through familiar territory with more, not less, conviction and enthusiasm" (*Preaching,* p. 162).

Preaching is not exhausted by Craddock's homiletics of recognition, for buried within the *nod* of recognition is the *shock* of recognition. Consistently effective preaching, he believes, will convey within it the shock of recognition. But, that shock is always latent within the nod, and without the latter, there will be no shock at all, but only anger. Such a negative reaction is almost inevitable, and results from one association of the shock with "the messenger and not with the message."[16] And again, for this shock to occur effectively, Craddock insists that considerable attention be given to details. His refrain-like admonition is for the preacher to stay in the story longer. "The power is in the details."[17] For the hearer to be addressed, convicted, or motivated calls for a prior awareness of the familiarity of the story, an assent to it, and a nod of recognition. Then, the shock can occur when that person realizes that he or she is "the one called, the one addressed, the one guilty, the one responsible, the one commissioned" (*Preaching,* p. 160). But without the antecedent "Amen," such a shock will not be experienced, for the story will not be recognized as my story.

This dynamic involving the interpretation of listeners is as fundamental to the process of sermon preparation as is the interpretation of the scripture. In fact, any movement from exegesis directly to preaching is inappropriate to the extent that it circumvents an evaluation of the congregational context for that preaching. Two distinct foci, therefore, are seen by Craddock as essential to effective preaching: one related to listeners and their personal and social contexts and the other related to the biblical text and its historical, literary, and theological contexts (*Preaching,* p. 85). Hence, he concludes:

> The practical question, long discussed by homileticians, has to
> do with whether one begins with the text or with the people in
> sermon preparation. . . . [But] in the movement here
> recommended, the experience is not of a trip from text to
> people or from people to text. . . . Both are actively involved
> (*AOW*, p. 132).

The listeners and the text must both be interpreted, with
canons of interpretation appropriate to each respective
context. What results, then, is a message which has
successfully negotiated the distance between the biblical past
and the contemporary pastoral situation. What has not
resulted yet, Craddock insists, is a sermon, for the methodology for designing a sermon is distinct from those processes
which have been utilized to interpret text and listeners
(*Preaching*, p. 153).

An overriding concern for homiletical method for Fred
Craddock is that of sermonic movement. Although sermons
may take a myriad of shapes, they tend to move generally in
one of two basic directions—along either deductive or
inductive patterns of thought. While the liabilities of the
former seem to clearly rule out a continuation of those
deductive patterns, an inductive approach embodies a
number of values which commend it as a living option in
homiletical method. The inductive method of preaching is
founded on a central conviction held by Craddock: that the
congregation on Sunday morning should be permitted to
take the same inductive trip that brought the preacher to the
pulpit and be granted the freedom to arrive at its own
conclusion (*AOW*, p. 57). Such a trip is sermonically possible
and, in fact, may make the explicit statement of its conclusion
unnecessary. Moreover, if the people have made the
inductive trip with the preacher, then "it is *their* conclusion,
and the implication for their own situations is not only clear
but personally inescapable" (*AOW*, p. 57).

Exactly what constitutes an inductive sermon is not
answerable in as immediate a fashion as the identifying
characteristics of the old deductive approach. There is for
Fred Craddock no one normative sermonic structure which

115

will predictably mark an effective sermon. In fact, he cautions, "a sermon is defined more by content and purpose than by form" (*Preaching,* p. 170). Nevertheless, there are a number of formal considerations which need to be taken into account if one is to preach inductively. Initially, though, two qualities are identified which serve to bring the nature of an inductive sermon more clearly into focus. In the first place, inductive preaching will be marked by attention to concrete experiences "not just in the introduction to solicit interest as some older theories held but throughout the sermon" (*AOW,* p. 61). Only through such a persistent focus on concrete experience will the listeners be enabled to identify with the preacher's message and with the journey leading to that destination. Second, inductive preaching will respect the listener by a sermonic movement which extends "the right to participate in that movement and arrive at a conclusion that is his own, not just the speaker's" (*AOW,* p. 62). In this respect, inductive preaching acknowledges the priesthood of all believers by inviting the congregation to come to its own conclusions regarding God's Word for them. To the contrary, a deductive approach would seem to be an *a priori* denial of this formation principle. The inductive process, Craddock states, insists that the preacher retain a certain "lack of exhaustiveness in the sermon. . . . [and] resist the temptation to tyranny of ideas rather than democratic sharing" (*AOW,* p. 64).

Inductive method in preaching will be effective to the extent that a number of qualities are present within the sermon. Given their presence the preacher is then released to focus more specifically on formal and organizational considerations. Craddock lists these as follows:

1. Movement. Inductive method in preaching subordinates structure to movement to the extent that the former may not even be noticeable by the congregation. Furthermore, inductive preaching demands that the form or outline used consistently move "from the present experience of the hearers to the point at which the sermon will leave [the congregation] to their own decisions and conclusion" (*AOW,*

p. 146). The beginning point in sermon preparation, consequently, is not with the introduction, but the conclusion. And the completed sermon will be a journey from the jumping off place which deals seriously with the thoughts and feelings of the hearers, to a conclusion in which that human situation is seen in the light of the presence of Christ. The message itself is the end of the sermon, arrived at by both preacher and people.

For this inductive movement to occur, however, the persistent challenge to the preacher is to create a sense of anticipation and sustain it. In fact, Craddock states, evoking such anticipation becomes "a primary burden of movement in a sermon" (*Preaching*, p. 166). The hearer's attention in an inductive sermon is much more critical than in the old deductive approach, since the message is the terminus of the sermon and not its point of origination. Not only will interest need to be maintained in order for both preacher and congregation to arrive at the sermon's conclusion, but the quality of anticipation also serves "to prepare the hearer's mood or mind set to grasp and participate in the central idea when it comes" (*AOW*, p. 151).

While there are numerous ways in which the quality of anticipation is sustained throughout a sermon, Craddock highlights the following three: First, the oral character of preaching is a vital element in the maintenance of sermonic interest and movement. Preaching is not a literary medium, and the rhetoric of preaching must be that of oral address. Second, Craddock suggests that in preparation the preacher sequentially list in tersely worded phrases the ideas of the sermon and then ask of this series of thoughts, "Does the material move along, evoking ideas and sustaining anticipation until the end?" (*AOW*, p. 155) Third, a similar scrutiny should search out transitional movements in the sermon denoted by such words as "and," "therefore," and "beyond this" (*AOW*, p. 156). These transitional markers should be well identified by the preacher since they will serve "as pegs on which to hang series of ideas, preserving the hard-won flow of material" (*AOW*, p. 156).

2. Unity. Not only must a sermon have movement as a primary characteristic, it must also have a unity within which that movement is grounded. "The contribution to the movement and power of a sermon made by the restraint of a single idea can hardly be overstated" (*AOW*, p. 100). Inductive sermons will not have points, but will have a point, the message toward which all of the material will tend. Therefore, it is essential that the preacher be able to clearly articulate the main idea of the sermon in a single sentence. Such a statement, for Craddock, is the appropriate and necessary outcome of the twin processes of scriptural and congregational interpretation. It is also to be maintained throughout the process of sermon preparation as the ground of the sermon's unity.

The governing theme serves on one hand as a magnet to attract appropriate material to the sermon in an ordered sequence. On the other hand, the statement will constantly serve as a guardian against the introduction of extraneous or potentially distracting material. Nothing can be more disastrous for a sermon than an illustration that arrogantly masters rather than serves. The sermonic theme will filter out such arrogant material *(AOW*, p. 101). The main idea will also serve to enhance the delivery of the sermon itself. Confident of the unity of the material, the preacher can enter the pulpit knowing that the sermon has a destination and that its various ideas and illustrations will build to a conclusion. Finally, the seminal idea of the sermon is needed because only such a grasp of the sermon's purpose and destination can release the imagination of the preacher, sustaining interest and even excitement. The imaginative faculties of the preacher will not remain focused and fruitful unless this crucial sermonic unity is maintained.

3. Imagination. Images are distinct from illustrations, according to Fred Craddock, the latter serving an ornamental function while the former are "essential to the form and inseparable from the content of the entire sermon" (*AOW*, p. 80). They are not to be confined to the introduction or inserted into the body of the sermon to pick up interest, nor are they susceptible to replacement by concepts. Within a person's imaginative consciousness, images "are replaced not by concepts but by other images, and that quite slowly" (*AOW*, p. 78). Since images function to recreate the way life is experienced, their function in both preparing and hearing a sermon is decisive. The minister will need an empathetic imagination, both to interpret the congregation and to form the sermon so that it reflects the realities of the listeners' life experience.

The question now becomes for Craddock how the preacher's images are "formed in the imagination of his hearers with clarity and force sufficient to effect changes in attitudes, values, and life directions"(*AOW*, p. 92). Several principles, he notes, are operative in this process of imaginative communication. First, it is important that the images be taken from real life, "cast in forms recognizable as real and possible" (*AOW*, p. 92). Then, the language used in the pulpit needs to be as concrete as possible, evoking immediate and familiar sensory experience. Generalized language—e.g., speaking of "holy matrimony" rather than imaging a specific wedding—serves to distance listeners from life and thereby severely reduces a sermon's effectiveness. The effectiveness and power of language employed in preaching are eroded also when adjectives and adverbs are over-used. Parenthetically, such use robs the hearers of their own judgments regarding the ideas and images. Craddock also admonishes the preacher to "avoid all self-conscious interruptions in narration and description" (*AOW*, p. 95). These interjections not only jar the vital sense of sermonic movement but serve to quash the congregation's imaginative faculties in favor of a focus on the preacher. Finally, in order for images to be effectively shared, the language used in preaching must be that of the preacher and not of someone else or of an assumed "pulpit personality." This is a call, Craddock states, "for the vernacular in the pulpit" (*AOW*, p. 96). Employment of these three principles is essential to the task of conveying the concrete realities of life within an inductive sermon. The principles also serve to heighten the empathetic imagination of the preacher so that impression precedes expression.

To have dealt effectively with the issue of unity, movement, and concrete imagery still does not provide a sermon with a specific form. Actually, Craddock observes, there is no one pattern to which preaching should inevitably conform. Yet the shape a sermon takes is not an inconsequential issue; rather, "the form itself is active, contributing to what the speaker wishes to say and do, sometimes no less persuasive than the content itself" (*Preaching,* p. 172). Form and content, then, are interrelated and interdependent. With an inductive approach to preaching, though, Craddock sets considerable stake on sermonic forms which will evoke and sustain congregational interest. The structure of a sermon will determine "the degree of participation demanded of the hearers" (*Preaching,* p. 174), and deductive preaching's inability to invite congregational participation is one of its primary deficiences. He reminds us that if the message is given first, with supportive material following the conclusions, the congregation is assumed to be passive throughout the process. Among the variety of forms available to the preacher, the goal is to choose those "that are both adequate and congenial to the message and the experience to be generated by the sermon" (*Preaching,* p. 176).

An increasingly popular approach among ministers, Craddock notes, is to derive the form of the sermon from the biblical text which provided the sermon's message. Not only does this approach provide the preacher with variety in sermonic forms, but it also helps insure a fundamental integrity to preaching by deriving both the message and design of the sermon from the same biblical source. Especially in situations where the sermon is based on a biblical narrative, Craddock encourages the preacher to achieve this congruence of form and message. "Why should I take something that comes to me as a parable," he asks, "and preach it as an outline?"[18] There are limitations to this approach, perhaps related to the non-narrative character of a good deal of the biblical material, but the unity and movement of a sermon are optimized when sermonic form is grounded in the literary form of a biblical text.

Finally, some forms have endured through long periods of the church's preaching, and it behooves the contemporary preacher to renew acquaintance with these homiletical traditions. The validity of forms which have persisted in the tradition is based, for Craddock, upon their persistently demonstrated ability to carry "the burden of truth with clarity, thoroughness, and interest" (*Preaching,* p. 176). This storehouse of readily available forms from the past include such standards as:

> "Explore, explain, apply
> The problem, the solution
> ....
> Either/or
> Both/and
> ....
> Ambiguity, clarity
> Major premise, minor premise, conclusion
> ....
> From the lesser, to the greater" (*Preaching,* p. 177).

While these examples include obviously deductive as well as inductive models, their value is shown in their persistence throughout church tradition and in their ability to offer the preacher a variety of sermon structures. Moreover, a varied diet of sermon patterns is critical if congregational interest is to be maintained. "No form is so good that it does not eventually become wearisome to both listener and speaker" (*Preaching,* p. 177). The preacher's alternatives regarding sermonic form, then, involve either the selection of a form—from the biblical text or homiletical tradition—or the creation of a form more immediately in accord with inductive principles.

In spite of the normative character of an inductive approach to biblical interpretation and congregational interpretation, the question of sermonic form remains open for the preacher. Both deductive as well as inductive approaches remain available and effective for preaching. The enduring issue for Fred Craddock, however, is the adequacy and congeniality of the sermonic form to the message lying at the heart of the sermon. Biblical preaching, then, will not so much focus on form as on the appropriateness of any sermonic form with regard to that sermon's message and its expression of the gospel.

Evaluation

Fred Craddock is for many a patriarch among those who have struggled for the renewal of preaching. *As One Without Authority* has been in print for fifteen years now; yet it remains both valid in its assessment of the old homiletic and prophetic in its outline of the issues for reform. Craddock's new work, *Preaching,* will be of help to a great many pastors and to generations of seminary students in their courses and preaching. Moreover, Fred Craddock is a preacher, too! He not only teaches the craft of preaching well, but demonstrates regularly that he has ably mastered this craft in his own ministry.

Among the many strengths evidenced in Craddock's writings, several have clear implications for an inquiry into homiletic method. First, he has not wavered in his insistence that preaching be *biblical* preaching. Responsible exegesis of the text is not an option, Craddock believes, and he uses his own expertise as a New Testament scholar to model the pastor's necessary work of interpretation.[19] This insistence on an attentive listening to the text exposes one of deductive preaching's most serious flaws, its regular misuse of the text. On the other hand, such a hearing of Scripture is, for Craddock, a necessary as well as felicitous aspect of the inductive approach to preaching.

Sensitive and insightful attention to the function of language also marks his research. While he is an honest reporter of the crisis in language, the linguistic analysis of Martin Heidegger and modern literary analysis are seen by

Craddock as providing a valuable foundation for a new homiletic. At the level of praxis, though, the implications for the language of preaching are both positive and helpful. The emphasis on a certain economy and discipline in language from the pulpit is an admonition which many preachers still need to hear and heed. Interestingly, this attention to the language of preaching also focuses on deductive preaching's tendency to moralize the gospel. The "ought," "must," and "should" hortatory which still afflicts the American pulpit is untenable as true biblical preaching expressed in a language congenial to the gospel.

One of the most valuable insights for homiletic method is Craddock's pastoral emphasis on the role of the assembly. The preacher must listen to the congregation as well as the biblical text. Without the former, a sermon becomes a positivistic restatement of scriptural "truth," but is not really biblical preaching. For an inductive approach, the real, lived experience of those within the community of faith is essential to the formation of the sermon and, in conjunction with the text, provides the sermon's message. Deductive preaching's use of life situations to "illustrate" themes and topics violates the integrity of the congregation's participation in the formation of the sermon. Its experience is essential to preaching, not an ornament to it.

Finally, Craddock has consistently maintained that preaching must have a persistent sense of movement within its sermonic form. For him as much as for Lowry, preaching without movement is a homiletical mortal sin. While there can be any number of forms through which the inductive method can come to fruition, the resulting sermon will always move in a way which sustains congregational interest and allows the hearers to arrive at a common destination. Craddock is accurate in his analysis that the deductive method precludes authentic movement within the sermon. There may be some movement within each "point," but the overall effect is as static as moths pinned to a corkboard.

The liabilities of the inductive method as espoused by Fred Craddock center on issues related to hermeneutics and sermonic form. A cluster of questions surrounds that shift in methodology when preaching ceases to interpret the text and begins to select or create a form for the sermon. The first of these issues relates to the "distance" experienced between the text and the interpreter. There is certainly an awareness that a sense of distance emerges when an exegete deals responsibly with a text—Craddock sees this realization as a necessary stage for the process of interpretation. His assumption that an exegetical living with the text serves to overcome the distance encountered earlier is, however, problematic. In fact, certain types of biblical form seem to be highly resistant to such an outcome (apocalyptic literature, miracles and signs, and the resurrection/ascension accounts, for example). Even the parable form, of which Craddock is particularly fond, has proven to be resistant to conventional historical-critical interpretation, given its "main idea" hermeneutic bias.[20] Although reference is made to the contributions of literary criticism, it is difficult to identify how this alternative approach to the text figures into Craddock's hermeneutics or affects his homiletic method.

A second issue which relates to both hermeneutics and sermonic form is that of thematic unity. Fred Craddock is quite explicit in his latest work that the end product of the interpretation of the text and the congregation is a "message" which then will become the *telos* for the movement and form of the sermon. What happens, one must ask, when an interpreter encounters a pericope which simply refuses such ideational reduction (this being the case precisely with the parables and probably with other narrative material such as the Johannine signs)? Either the preacher must impose a thematic on the text from outside, or be threatened with a collapse in sermonic unity. The literary critics of biblical narrative and their preaching-as-story fellow travelers have demonstrated that plot serves more effectively as a principle of homiletical control than the notion of a text's message, at least regarding narrative literature in Scripture. The implications of this insight for homiletic method are undeveloped by Craddock, however, and the "weak link" in his approach remains the assumption that the interpretive payoff of every text is a proposition which then becomes the homiletic payoff of every sermonic form. Viewed from this perspective, the distance between a homiletics of induction and that of deduction closes considerably. Both seem to be bound to a rationalist hermeneutic, notwithstanding the inductive method's clear advantages in sustaining congregational interest and involvement in the sermon.

A final issue relates specifically to homiletic form. The inductive method yields a sermon whose form and movement are readily detectable to the hearer. "Surrounded" (pp. 126-30) is a clear example of Fred Craddock's deft employment of his inductive method as well as the correlative norms of language and imagery. An inductive sermon is a relatively easy species for the attentive listener to spot! Yet by the conclusion of his discussion of form, Craddock has also offered as viable options a series of forms from homiletic tradition, most of which are variations on the deductive model. What is confusing to the reader/preacher here is that after so much attention to biblical interpretation and the contemporary situation, the message of the sermon may still gain form through multiple choices: by way of the shape of the text, through some sort of inductive movement, or from deductive models provided in the tradition. Perhaps the problem here is the rather sharp delineation between exegetical and homiletic method. What if hermeneutics informed more immediately both the interpretation of the text and the emergence of homiletic form and movement? The preaching-as-storytelling homileticians have demonstrated that this strategy can apply quite effectively to specific narrative biblical literature. It may well be, then, that Fred Craddock is most vulnerable with regard to a hermeneutic which inadequately provides for the alignment of scriptural interpretation and sermonic formation.

SURROUNDED

Fred Craddock

ACTS 26:12-18 (RSV)

"Thus I journeyed to Damascus with the authority and commission of the chief priests. At midday, O king, I saw on the way a light from heaven brighter than the sun, shining round me and those who journeyed with me. And when we had all fallen to the ground, I heard a voice saying to me in the Hebrew language, 'Saul, Saul, why do you persecute me? It hurts you to kick against the goads.' And I said, 'Who are you, Lord?' And the Lord said, 'I am Jesus, whom you are persecuting. But rise and stand upon your feet; for I have appeared to you for this purpose, to appoint you to serve and bear witness to the things in which you have seen me and to those in which I will appear to you, delivering you from the people and from the Gentiles—to whom I send you to open their eyes, that they may turn from darkness to light and from the power of Satan to God, that they may receive forgiveness of sins and a place among those who are sanctified by faith in me."

I don't know if you were listening very carefully to the reading of the text, but I was. And frankly I felt some distance between the text and myself. It was not the fairly common distance of unfamiliarity. I am familiar with the story the text narrates. Three times in the book of Acts and once in a letter, the letter to the Galatians, the story of Paul's conversion and call to the ministry has been given. Saul, or better known as Paul, was a persecutor of Christians. The accounts agree he was on his way to Damascus, Syria, in pursuit of his ugly business when his life was turned around. He was in the company of several others, and about noon as they approached the city he saw a light, and out of the light, a person. He heard a sound and from the sound, a voice. As a result of that experience, he was turned from dealing death to the Christians to a life of missionary work on behalf of the gospel. That work took him to Syria, Turkey, Greece, and finally, Italy. I know the story and you know the story. We experience no distance of unfamiliarity here.

The distance I feel is rather that of being unable to identify with the story. Here is a man on the wrong track and he is halted by vision and by voice. In front of him is the person of Jesus of

Nazareth and behind him, according to this text, moves some unnamed pressure, which is prompting him and goading him toward what is right. "It is hard for you to kick against the goads." In other words, he is surrounded, unmistakably, by the influences of God.

Now the distance I feel is simply this: God has, in my experience, been much more timid, applying very little pressure at all. In fact, at times I hardly know He's there. Now don't get me wrong. I believe that God communicates. But my experience of His communication is that of whispers, not shouts. And sometimes, the whisper is a very low whisper; in fact, sometimes I'm not even sure of His word or of His will. I believe He acts. But when you are the only one around who saw what He did you begin to wonder if He really did it. For example: sometime after recovering from an illness, say, "God restored my health," and say it among your friends and relatives. Do you suppose you'll get strange glances? Why? You do believe God restored your health, but it was not obvious, was it? Or, after some major turn in your road, say, "God answered my prayers." And say it in the midst of friends and relatives and see what response there is. Probably they are thinking, "You were always lucky." Or, "What a coincidence that that should happen," but they cannot identify with God answering prayers.

There are some people who feel that their lives have been so victimized that the problem they have with God is His fairness. Such has not been my case. My problem with God is His timidity, His quietness. Even on the most religious occasions He stands back in the shadows. Ask the people around you, "Do you think God is here today?" Some of them will say, "Of course, He is." Others will say, "I hope He is." Others say, "Well, I never thought about it." Others will say, "I'm not into that kind of stuff."

The story in the text for today impresses this matter on my mind. How can I think about it? Is it true that God once encountered people with vision and voice unmistakably loud and clear, but now He has changed His strategy? Or maybe He still does that for those who have faith, and I simply do not have the faith? Or is it that the writer who reports these things in the Bible has misrepresented the case?

Certainly it is helpful to take time to realize that there are huge differences in the language writers use to relate a faith story. In the book of Acts, for instance, it is quite obvious that the writer narrates history as God's story. His accounts are given as though God obviously were the principle character in everything that happened. And he projects it all on wide screen and in technicolor. For instance, he tells the story of the death of Herod Agrippa. Now Herod Agrippa died of gout and the general effects of severe intemperance. However, the writer of the book of Acts says God sent worms and they ate him. In the book of Acts there is the story of Christian missionaries being released from prison due to a big earthquake. The writer says God sent an earthquake. There are visions everywhere, there are angels everywhere. That's the way the writer tells the story.

Now in contrast, the apostle Paul, in his letters, very seldom speaks of anything unusual. He is very low on visions and miracles. In fact, the story we have just read about his own conversion and call to be an apostle, he himself tells very very quietly. In the letter to the Galatians he says, "When God was pleased to reveal his son in me." That's quite different from saying there was a voice and a light and the figure of Jesus. He tells it much more reservedly, without the loud voice, without the bright colors. This is not to say that Paul was less Christian. This is not to say that Paul had less faith. Part of the difference lies simply in the way you tell something.

It is also helpful to read the text very carefully. We will discover that even in passages like this one before us, passages that seem to be full of visions and voices, things are not as obvious as they seem. For instance, Paul went to Damascus in the company of several others, but the experience on the way to Damascus was his alone. Those who were with him did not see Jesus of Nazareth. Those who were with him did not hear a message from Jesus of Nazareth; only Paul heard it. How are we to understand this? One way to understand it is that even in those marvelous, extraordinary pasages like this, the writer still makes it clear that only the ears and eyes of faith get the message. Recall the scene in the Gospel of John when Jesus lifted his voice to God and said, "Father, glorify your name." John says the voice of God said, "I have glorified it and I will glorify it again." Some standing around thought it thundered. Others said an angel spoke to him. What really happened? According to the writer, much depended on the kind of ear you brought to the occasion.

This perspective is generally true of the Bible. Those marvelous stories of the miracles of Jesus which may seem so persuasive to a Christian reader—remember they are told in such a way that some people standing nearby could come immediately after an exorcism or a healing and say to Jesus, "Show us a sign that you are really one with this authority." It is easy to say, "How blind can anyone be? Where were they? Didn't they just see what happened?" Obviously they did not. Sometimes we tend to criticize unreasonably the people who did not see and hear, when actually what they missed was not really all that obvious. I am convinced that God has always whispered, and that He has been heard only by those who lean forward. Of course, what faith has heard, faith has then shouted, but with all that shouting we have to remember that to the hearer it is always a whisper. Isn't it the case that God has always stood in the shadows? When the faith sees Him, faith describes Him in bold colors, but we should understand that there is always plenty of room for reasonable people to say, "I do not think He was there." In other words, God does not overwhelm us. He leaves everyone room to say no, so that when one does say yes, it will be a freely decided and responsible yes.

Having said that, I must go on to affirm that faith *does* see, *does* hear, and we are still, in these post-biblical times, surrounded by God's presence. If you don't believe it, just go out and read the face of nature. He has never left himself without witness. This is not true only when the snow falls fresh upon the earth. This is not true only when you are looking at a lake glistening in the sun, or see ripe peaches heavy on the tree, or a newborn white-faced calf standing for the first time on wobbly legs. This is not true only when you see yellow pumpkins asleep among the sentinel shocks of grain, or view the evening sun sizzling into the sea, or flying clouds on a frosty night, or green meadows turning somersaults of joy. Read the face of nature in barren places, too, and you will discover there is more life, even in the crack of a sidewalk, than you ever noticed before. There is more life stirring in the desert than the speeding tourist ever sees. Not one square inch of the universe is so deprived or neglected but what, upon looking closely, you can see His initials in the lower right hand corner.

Or read your own heart. Take a stroll down the back roads and along the rivers of your mind. Are you looking for anyone? Our fathers in the faith said He made us for Himself; we are seeking after Him, hoping to find Him. The poet of ancient Greece, without the inspiration of Jewish or Christian Scripture, was still able to sing, "In him we live and move and have our being." No blinding vision, no heavenly voice, to be sure, but it is real nevertheless. God still surrounds us, even though He Himself may be whispering and standing in the shadow.

Or look around you. Look at the persons beside you or across the table from you. Do you see anything unusual about them? Of course, you do. For when God had created everything else, pine cones, squirrels, and everything, He said, "That is good." But it was only when He made those people beside you and across from you that He said, "This is my own image, my own likeness." Had you noticed that before? You can see it, too, when you are looking in the mirror; that is, if you look carefully.

Sure, we're still surrounded; you just have to look, and listen. You say that's not enough? Well, permit me one last word. No one has ever really seen God, but there was a man who dwelt among us, a man who was so transparent, so free of selfish grasping for himself, that many looked upon Jesus of Nazareth and said they saw God. Is that not enough? If it is final proof you seek, we have none. We can only speak of what we have seen and heard.

NOTES

1. Fred B. Craddock, *As One Without Authority* (Nashville: Abingdon Press, 1979), p. 54. (Hereafter *AOW*.)
2. Fred B. Craddock, *Preaching* (Nashville: Abingdon Press, 1985), p. 100. (Hereafter *Preaching*.)
3. See ibid., pp. 52 ff. for the author's analysis of the theological considerations related to silence and Word of God.
4. The reader is reminded that this particular analysis of the crisis in language was written during the latter years of the 1960s, when the "death of God" controversy was of major importance, and prior to most of the hermeneutical advances in the understanding of parable and metaphor which occurred during the following decade.
5. Fred B. Craddock, "The Sermon and the Uses of Scripture," *Theology Today* 42, no. 1 (April 1985), p. 7. (Hereafter *SUS*.)
6. Fred B. Craddock, "Recent New Testament Interpretation and Preaching," *The Princeton Seminary Bulletin* 66, no. 1 (October 1973), p. 76. (Hereafter *RNT*.)
7. Ibid., p. 77. Craddock's "new angle of vision" implies approaches to the text which can traverse the distance between the contemporary church and the biblical world, not annihilate that distance. It is neither desirable nor possible, he believes, "to collapse their difference in contrived harmony" (*SUS*, p. 8).
8. Fred B. Craddock, "Occasion-Text-Sermon," *Interpretation* 35, no. 1 (January 1981), p. 60. On the other hand, Craddock notes that having a text at the beginning of the process does not always result in biblical preaching. "Some preachers start with a text and then visit every city but Nazareth" (ibid).
9. Ibid., p. 63.
10. Fred B. Craddock, "Preaching as Story-telling" (Paper delivered at Lecture II, Furman University Pastor's School, Greenville, South Carolina, June 3, 1980).
11. Fred B. Craddock, "The Commentary in the Service of the Sermon," *Interpretation* 36, no. 4 (October 1982), p. 386.
12. Ibid., p. 387. In this article Fred Craddock more precisely defines the sequence by which various resources are to be consulted. Following the first reading time on Monday, lexicons, Bibles, dictionaries, and theological workbooks of the Bible are utilized on Tuesday. Wednesday is commentary day, while Thursday's work turns the preacher to commentaries dealing more immediately with the implications of the text for the present situation. Friday's resources will be of various types and will all focus on the contemporary context for preaching (pp. 386-87).
13. Craddock, "Occasion-Text-Sermon," p. 64. See *Preaching*, pp. 107-10 for a more extensive consideration of the issues related to establishing the text.
14. Ibid., p. 65.
15. Fred B. Craddock, "Preaching and the Nod of Recognition" (Paper delivered at The Hickman Lectures I, Duke University Divinity School Convocation, Durham, North Carolina, October 29, 1984).

16. Fred B. Craddock, "Preaching and the Shock of Recognition" (Paper delivered at The Hickman Lectures II, Duke University Divinity School Convocation, Durham, North Carolina, October 30, 1984).

17. Ibid.

18. Fred B. Craddock, "Preaching as Storytelling" (Paper delivered at Lecture III, Furman University Pastor's School, Greenville, South Carolina, June 3, 1980).

19. We have come to expect regular contributions from Fred Craddock in the areas of exegetical and homiletical studies. Included among these works is Fred Craddock and Leander Keck, *Proclamation: Aids for Interpreting the Lessons of the Church Year, Series B.* (Philadelphia: Fortress Press, 1976).

20. See Richard L. Eslinger, "Preaching the Parables and the Main Idea," *The Perkins School of Theology Journal* 36, no. 4 (Fall 1983), pp. 24-32.

5

DAVID BUTTRICK

A Phenomenological Method

The old rational homiletics is obsolete. "For nearly three hundred years, preaching has been trapped in a rationalist 'bind,' "[1] observes David Buttrick. But the conditions that made for its viability no longer stand. Every dimension of homiletics—biblical interpretation, hermeneutics, language, theology, the liturgical context, and even human consciousness—has changed radically; yet Sunday after Sunday points, topics, and propositions remain the quest of not just a few preachers. A new homiletic will be formed at the intersection of these new realities, but first it is important to obtain an overview of the interesting history of the old conceptual preaching and briefly ask of it, What is wrong here?

When the Reformation hardened into a post-Reformation Scholasticism, preaching too was molded into a formal and rigid schema. The sermon predictably dealt with "careful understanding, explication, and application"[2] of the biblical text. By the end of the Enlightenment, this form had evolved into one still surviving in many pulpits today: "An *introduction* was followed by the *text*, which in turn was reduced to a propositional *topic*, which was developed in a series of *'points'* (often categorical), before the sermon ended in a *conclusion*" (*IP*, p. 47). Following the emergence of this propositional, "point" oriented sermon, preaching underwent an alteration by what Buttrick labels "pop-Schleiermacher." Locating religious truth within human subjectivity, the preacher began

---

David Buttrick is professor of homiletics, Vanderbilt University Divinity School, Nashville, Tennessee.

to seek ideas derived from personal/pastoral experience, prior to searching Scripture for textual support or reproof. Typically, the sermon form then continued by explicating the main idea through a series of points. "The result," Buttrick notes, "is that now we have a romantic concept of 'inspiration' coupled with rational method, a mix found in most homiletic texts today" (*IP,* p. 47). During the twentieth century, Harry Emerson Fosdick would modify the model by beginning with a specific personal problem and by then relating it to some general religious truths often derived from Scripture. Predictably, the sermon would then conclude after an extended illustration (*IP,* p. 48).

Whether the particular expression is post-Reformation scholastic or twentieth-century situational, rational homiletics has been marked by categorical development and a focus on "objective truth." Buttrick detects a strong kinship between the development of this rationalistic approach and early scientific method. The former "does seem to parody scientific procedure in which an object is isolated for study and a general deduction is followed by descriptive statements" (*IP,* p. 47). What becomes problematic, however, is how the biblical Word is treated within a topical objective model of preaching. On one hand the very character of biblical language, filled as it is with story, image, and poetry, would seem to fight against the constraints of such a method. A conceptual scheme in fact will deal with such Scripture as "on-the-page inert language from which something may be removed and talked about" (*PCF,* p. 54). Interpretation by means of distillation inevitably removes narrative or poetic meaning "and those traveling shifts in thought that animate the scriptures" (*PCF,* p. 54). The Bible is reduced to a source book for objective propositions, its stories viewed simply as illustrations of an ideational world of religious truths.

As a correlate of this method of distillation, a conceptual homiletic also assumes that single texts can serve as the containers for these themes. A preacher will mount the pulpit with the "text" of the day already printed in the bulletin or announce as an objective the "breaking open of the text."

Texts are transformed into thematics and developed propositionally. But this hermeneutic clearly results in the importation of otherwise derived truths into a scriptural setting since, as Buttrick observes, "single verses seldom mean anything out of context" (*IP*, p. 47). When these truths and principles are traced to their extra-biblical source, moreover, it is soon evident that they are derived from the more general cultural ethos within which the preaching occurs. Evidence presents itself "that the habit of distilling 'truths' has flourished in eras when faith and culture are in synthesis, when there is a sense of vertical *analogia* alive in public mind" (*IP*, p. 55). An obsolescence will necessarily infect this rational homiletic when it persists well into a time when such cultural stasis and integration are no longer prevalent. To preach fixed topics and eternal truths within the contemporary culture is to insist that the listeners become Victorian before they can hear the gospel. But, of course, such cultural repristination is not really possible.

So the question becomes for David Buttrick, "What is the matter with homiletic method?" (*IP*, p. 46) The listeners are aware that preaching dwells on a level of language that is too general, rarely getting close enough to lived experience. And most hearers sense that "preaching" is synonymous with harmless, shallow declarations on virtues and feelings. It is too often "moralistic or pietistic and without depth" (*PCF*, p. 54). But the way out will not be through further modifications in the old topical approach, either by interjecting more elaborate story illustrations or heavier doses of "warm-fuzzy" subjectivity. Depth in preaching can be achieved, but the three-hundred-year-old tradition will need to come to an end, its forms and outlines the subject for study in the history of preaching, yet released from current praxis. The conditions necessary for a new homiletic have already come to pass, and the most significant of these factors, perhaps, is the new biblical studies.

The various expressions of rational homiletic method have all related to Scripture through what David Buttrick has labeled a "method of distillation." The biblical passage is reduced to a single theme and, methodologically, that reduction/distillation needs to occur before the sermon can be preached. Through such an approach, the text (pericope) has been viewed as a static field from which an idea is to be taken, "a still-life picture in which some*thing* may be found, object-like, to preach on" (*IP*, p. 49). Approaching Scripture with this distillation method is analogous to "explaining" Van Gogh's *Starry Night* by isolating and analyzing the church steeple, or one of the trees. What is by-passed is any attention to the composition of the work of art or its intention, to "what the picture wants to do."[3] Thus, in approaching the Lukan story of the centurion's slave (Luke 7:2-10), for example, a preacher dealing objectively with the passage will either isolate a verse as a "text"—"Say the word," "I am not worthy"—or distill a theme or general idea—"true worthiness," "the compassion of Jesus" *(FSH)*. What has been ignored, for Buttrick, are most of the elements which convey the passage's significance:

> The composition of the "picture," the narrative structure, the movement of the story, the whole question of what in fact the *passage* may want to preach. Above all, notice that the passage has been treated as a stopped, objective picture from which something may be taken out to preach on! (*IP*, p. 49)

Homiletically, Scripture is treated as a "static construct" from which an idea is distilled or a "text" is extracted.[4]

Recent literary-critical insights, however, have convincingly established that Scripture is not susceptible to objective preaching's method of distillation. Biblical passages are more like films than still-lifes; they "display movement of thought, event, or image" (*IP*, p. 53). This scriptural movement, moreover, is episodic and embodies some kind of sequential logic. The issue for the interpreter is, therefore, not to ask first "What did the passage mean?" but to inquire as to the logic of its plotted language.

Does the pericope reflect a "visual" logic or one of a narrative system? Or is there reversal or irony lurking in the passage's episodic movement? Literary-critical methodology has detected in biblical language both "mobile, plotted structures of meaning," and language that is performative in purpose (*PCF*, p. 54). Every pericope will have a moving structure of some sort which has both a logic and an intention. Of particular interest to the biblical interpreter, therefore, are the related concerns as to the *why* and *how* of a pericope's form. "Why was a particular form chosen? How does the form function?" (*IP*, p. 50) The "logic" of the passage will be evident through a structural analysis which will disclose the plotting of its episodes in sequence. These "systems of structural telling"—which may be most evident in narrative—"can be analyzed with literary categories—time, space, character, 'point-of-view' " (*IP*, p. 51). The form, story in this instance, will have a particular structure and movement expressed through a sequence of episodes of meaning. In the course of his analysis of the centurion's slave pericope, for example, Buttrick identifies the following episodes:

> Introduction: Servant ill
>
> "He is worthy"
> Merit: God and country
>
> "I am *not* worthy"
>
> "But, say the word"
> Authority
>
> "Not in Israel do I find faith."
> "But here"
>
> Conclusion: Servant well
> (FSH)

By plotting what has all the appearances of a miracle story, a much deeper issue is revealed. The text wants to move the hearer from an assumed theology of merit to one of grace (*FSH*). But such plotting of the episodes of a scripture's structure is not limited to narrative material alone. In fact, Buttrick insists, much of what is taken for "story" really consists solely of dialog. To the extent that all language "involves structured speaking, a sequence of ideas or images logically designed" (*IP*, p. 51), non-narrative material can also be plotted and its logic identified.

When a biblical passage's episodic movement is plotted, it will be discovered that the structure is moving through a theological field. This underlying "field of concern" is discovered "by analyzing separate episodes theologically" (*IP*, p. 52). Thus, the analysis of the plot of Luke 7:1-10 as well as an inquiry into the meaning of its respective episodes or movements reveals that the field of concern involves appeals to merit and grace. But that theological field will always remain the context for some plotted system of language and cannot be distilled into a static theme. As Buttrick notes, "we are still dealing with a theological field and a play—the play is crucial. . . . We mustn't lose it" (*FSH*). As these episodes of a pericope "play" within a field of concern, the interpreter notices that a hidden perspective begins to emerge. Texts embody something like a hermeneutical lens through which the writer views the subject and this perspective becomes "a submerged field in which the structures of a text move" (*IP*, p. 57). There is a "theo-logic" by which the author chooses the sequences of the episodes in a plot and the focus within each episode which is significant for the meaning of each structural element. Rather than asking the historical question, a preacher will need to ask questions of the logic of a pericope's structure and movement and of the hermeneutical focus of its underlying field of concern.

According to Buttrick, a further consideration for the preacher in interpreting a text is the issue of its "addressed world." What is meant by this are the "world constructs" that are shared by the social consciousness of the listeners (*IP*, p. 53). For example, "the parable of the workers and hours (Matt. 20:1-15) seems to presume that listeners have bought into a 'just' Deuteronomic world in which meritorious labors are rewarded by a record-keeping God; whereas the similitude of the mustard seed may address a mentality which anticipates the salvation of the pagans through Israel's triumph" (*IP*, p. 53). Both the speaker in the oral tradition and the redactor(s), then, will possess some focused sense of the "world" they are addressing.

Alongside David Buttrick's conviction that Scripture conveys meaning by moving plots of episodes within a field of concern, a further assessment of biblical language is made. Not only will the language of Scripture *say* something (have a message), it will *do* something as well. Buttrick is assuming that language is performative, "trying to do something to an attendant listening consciousness" *(FSH)*, and that this vital function of language pertains to almost all biblical language. He argues:

> In the ancient world spoken language was employed in more sophisticated ways than in our crumbling linear culture. First century folk grasped language like a tool, choosing form and style and structure to shape purpose. Thus biblical language is language designed to function in consciousness *(IP,* p. 54).

Biblical language is intentional; a pericope will want to function in the consciousness of the hearer in some way. Therefore, an interpreter is never finished with a text when a "message" has been found. For Buttrick, the central question becomes, What does the passage want to do?

The implications for preaching of this literary and phenomenological approach to Scripture (Buttrick labels it "patchwork phenomenology") are evident and immediate. Obviously, it will no longer do for the preacher to seize a "message" and then somewhat arbitrarily exploit some method or other to preach it. There is an intent to the language of Scripture which will be reflected in the intent of the sermon. For preaching to be biblical, it will seek faithfulness not only to the message of a text, but to its purpose expressed through its performative language. Raising this latter question of intention "may well mark the beginning of homiletical obedience" *(IP,* p. 58). Such obedience will be evidenced by preaching's attentiveness to how a text functions in the consciousness of its hearers, both as to its mobility and its performative language.

Preaching deals not only with the language of Scripture, but necessarily with the expression of that text in the language of the contemporary audience. People live in language as fish swim in water, and preaching will need to express the Word through a specific community's speech. What is problematic for preaching, however, is that the language is incredibly unstable at present, probably reflecting some fundamental reorientation in how language forms in human consciousness. Though not intended as an exhaustive symptomology of the crisis in language, Buttrick centers his attention on the following cultural and linguistic phenomena:

1. A dramatic shift is occurring in the amount of language in use. Over the past fifty years "we have sloughed off nearly half the vocabulary our forebears enjoyed. The trend, since 1960, is to multiply new words at a furious rate" (*PCF*, p. 51). Regarding the loss of language, Buttrick reports that of the 450,000 words in the *Webster's Dictionary* of 1935, only 150,000 remained in use by 1978. On the other hand, another 200,000 words have come into the language since 1950.[5]

2. The current linguistic shift is not solely a quantitative matter of losses and gains. Particularly as regards oral communication in groups (preaching), an equally dramatic qualitative shift has occurred as well. The performative power of "third person conceptual language" (like Lowry's spatial talk) is what is not functioning in oral communication to groups. Generic, conceptual words (mankind, patriotism, sin) no longer "form" in the group consciousness as well, if at all.[6] Preachers may lament this loss with even more feeling than the quantitative diminishment of the language, since so much of preaching unfortunately remains at this third person conceptual level of discourse. Such conceptual language may have functioned effectively during the era of the "pulpit giants," Buttrick admits, but it is no longer potent in today's preaching.

What has emerged with great force, though, is a new, vigorous language centering on image, metaphor, and story.

This language does form in consciousness today with immediacy and an awesome power *(IS)*. Any new homiletic should of necessity incorporate these factors into its methodology of preaching.

3. Specifically with reference to research about oral rhetoric, language is also functioning differently in consciousness. In oral communication, an audience needs nearly three minutes to achieve clarity concerning a single idea. The other side of the coin involves the shorter attention span of the hearers—it is difficult for a group to focus on an idea for more than three minutes. The result, Buttrick observes, is that "preachers find themselves in a peculiar bind: congregations need time to comprehend ideas, but they will not attend any idea for long" *(PCF,* p. 51). The window of time within which a constitutive element of a sermon must be developed and completed has become "desperately narrow" *(PCF,* p. 51).

If the new biblical studies of literary criticism have rendered the old homiletic obsolete, this radical shift in language also signals the end of objective preaching's life span. Even if rationalist, propositional preaching persists in some pulpits, that preaching will be devoid of linguistic potency. And since "faith comes from hearing" (Rom. 10:17 TEV), the old conceptual rhetoric will need to be jettisoned by a church intent on proclaiming God's Word. "Not since the collapse of the Greco-Roman world or the dissolution of the Medieval synthesis has there been such awesome reconstruction of language.[7] A faithful church will eagerly seek a new homiletic to accommodate such an upheaval in language and culture.

The kind of phenomenological analysis of language recommended by David Buttrick provides a mirror for social consciousness. Public language, in fact, may be one of the most important vehicles by which this shared consciousness is expressed and studied. To the extent, therefore, that language is undergoing such awesome shifts, the phenomenal world of consciousness is experiencing flux as well. Not only is rapid change occurring, however, it is also evident that social experience "at the ragged tag-end of the twentieth century is nothing if it is not complex, ambiguous, and full of shadowy mystery (*PCF*, p. 54). Preaching will need to be alert not only to these striking linguistic shifts, but also to the depths and complexities of human experience. A conceptual approach to preaching, though, is unable to engage these profound experiences at the level where image and metaphor abound.

There is one other major implication drawn by Buttrick from this relationship of language to a "social world." Language's disclosure of the shared social world calls into question a central premise of modern preaching—that the object of the sermon is to address individuals *as* individuals. For thirty years, Buttrick asserts, "the American pulpit has addressed either the internal one-to-one self—the triumph of the therapeutic—or it has preached a one-to-one morality for individuals."[8] The difficulty with this approach, however, is that the object of such preaching—the one-to-one self—does not exist. Ironically, "in the name of relevance we have preached to an abstraction."[9] If language reveals the room of consciousness to be papered with the slogans, images, values, and symbols of a shared social world, then preaching which assumes that either salvation or holiness can be strictly an individual matter is seriously misguided. Buttrick cautions, though, that this critique of the "personalism" of the American pulpit is by no means a vindication of the old social gospel. It, too, preached in the name of relevance, but also preached to an abstraction. "The social gospeler preached to a world without a self, the pietist preached to a self without a world."[10] Biblical preaching needs to avoid both traps, by refusing to engage in static abstractions. In place of isolated selves and a fixed God, the biblical preacher will witness to "the relating of an on-the-move purposeful God with his lag-behind pilgrim people" (*IP*, p. 55).

The issue of homiletic method, for David Buttrick, begins with a question—"If pericopes are moving language, if they imply a 'world,' have structured significance and performative purpose, what will a 'biblical' preaching be?" (*IP*, p. 55)

The answer, he believes, does not lie in the direction of separating exegetical and homiletical method. Labeling himself a "homiletic exegete," Buttrick now turns to a homiletic theory which seeks to couple lived experience with structural understandings within hermeneutic consciousness.[11] A sermon needs to be formed to function in consciousness much as thoughts themselves form, hence a "phenomenological" method. The object for the congregation is not so much to *hear* the sermon as to have it form in their consciousness *(FTS)*. Hence, the preacher should be asking of the language of the sermon the same question asked of the biblical text—what is its intention, its performative purpose? The sermon "should be designed to locate as action in hermeneutic consciousness where language and the images of human experience meet" *(IP,* p. 55). The issue of strategy will remain of primary importance in preaching, therefore. How language functions to form meaning in consciousness is crucial to every sermon.

If language is to function with immediacy within hermeneutic consciousness, then several of the conceptual approach strategies to preaching are immediately ruled out. Since preaching should attempt to imitate the movement of consciousness, topics cannot be objectified and talked about. "Preaching should be a speaking *of* Scripture," Buttrick insists, "and not *about* Scripture" *(IP,* p. 55). There is a subject-object dichotomy established when the sermon talks about a text, which precludes the replicating of that text's performative purpose in the mind of the hearers. Moreover, speaking about Scripture inevitably distances the congregation from the "world" of the text. Assemblies are urged to study, to believe, or to appreciate Scripture, but the invitation to enter its movement and intention is not extended. Preaching, then, needs to refrain from any strategy, including talking about Scripture, which prevents the sermon from happening in the minds of the people.

Speaking *of* rather than *about* Scripture also involves mobile systems of language in the sermon as well as the text. Since the sermon will need to function much as consciousness travels, the mobility of its language and structure became critical. Having noted that what is encountered in Scripture is "movement of thought or event or image by some 'logic' " (*IP*, p. 55), the challenge for the preacher is to replicate the logic of that movement within the mind of the hearers. The sermon will not remain static; rather, its language will be designed to move in consciousness, fulfilling the intention latent in the biblical text. Moreover, this capability of preaching to not only communicate a message, but to make something happen, expresses with faithfulness the biblical understanding of conversion. Rather than a static model of vertical alignment between this "saved" person and a fixed God, Buttrick sees *metanoia* as transformation. If the language of preaching imitates hermeneutic consciousness, it has the capability of moving the hearer from one understanding to another *(FTS)*. A mobile system of language forming in consciousness, Buttrick notes, "has awesome power."[12]

This necessary mobility in sermonic structure is not adequately achieved, for David Buttrick, by conforming to a homiletics of storytelling. Not only is there not as much story in Scripture as the advocates of storytelling would have the church believe, but even when a biblical narrative is at stake, it is not necessary to be restricted to a narrative methodology in preaching. "The *how* and *why* of form is more important than the form itself," he observes (*IP*, p. 56). Rather than resorting to a narrative homiletic form, mobility is achieved by plotting sermon structure in much the same way the structure of the text was plotted. The logic of the biblical passage seen in the movement of its component episodes will be of immediate significance to the logic and mobility of the sermon, although "sermons need not follow the sequence of a particular passage slavishly" (*IP*, p. 56). Of more importance than a compulsive replication of the pericope's structure is faithfulness to its hermeneutic intention and performative purpose. "In preaching, deep structures and performative purposes take precedence over form" (*IP*, p. 56).

Sermon structure within a phenomenological method will achieve mobility through a sequence of episodes of meaning plotted according to some logic or intention. Such a moving structure will be plotted much as a narrative system moves; however, the episodes will relate to the logic of a wide variety of biblical literary forms. (For Buttrick, Pauline convictional logic can be plotted as readily as that of a synoptic parable.) The homiletical pay-off of this approach is that the structure of the sermon "ought to travel through congregational consciousness as a series of immediate thoughts, sequentially designed and imaged with technical skill so as to assemble in forming faith" (*IP,* pp. 55-56). Buttrick denotes these episodes of meaning or immediate thought as "moves." For him a sermon is a sequence of moves carefully designed to form in group consciousness according to the "theo-logic" of the biblical text. And since these moves must perform with reference to a plotted sequence, each in turn will need to form in the mind as a module of language.

Each move in a sermon, then, will have as a goal its formation in the consciousness of hearers. And since a move imitates the way understanding occurs in the mind, there is a need to develop within it both the conceptual dimension of meaning as well as imagery which conveys that meaning. Every idea elaborated into a move will need to be imaged "because an idea in abstract is no idea at all."[13] For preaching to form within the immediacy of thought rather than to be simply heard as words, this imagery will need to be concrete and connected to the lived experience of the hearers. Without the presence of such specific images, preaching has reverted to "talk about." "No one will know what I am talking about if I talk conceptually," Buttrick adds; "I've got to talk within the phenomenal 'stuff' of this world so people can see" *(PM).* On the other hand, images must be related with care to the conceptual structure of the move. They will need to relate not only to the meaning of a move, but to its structure as well. That is, a move whose conceptual expression relates to the world's propensity to shut out the gospel will utilize an image in which that closing out actually occurs.[14]

Images do not simply appear in the mind as phenomenal entities, they form in consciousness with a point of view, providing a kind of hermeneutic orientation. There is a perspectuality to our experience which is ubiquitous—we always find images being received with a point of view built into their meaning. Since a well-designed move in a sermon will form in the same way that thought travels in consciousness, the images within each move will provide an "angle of vision" from which they are to be experienced. Within the recent history of conceptual preaching, illustrations have been given with either no point of view or solely that of the preacher's own experience. But today, Buttrick observes, "human consciousness is multiperspectual" *(FTS)*, reflected for example in modern art or a televised rock concert. The old late-show movies with their fixed camera looking at moving actors seems oddly stilted to the modern consciousness. Topical preaching, however, will typically retain this fixed perspectuality in its use of illustration. Aiming for immediacy of formation in the group consciousness, the preacher today will need to build in a point of view with every image provided.

Since images will be interwoven with conceptual material within every move in the sermon, the possibility exists to design image systems which interact with each other throughout the sermonic structure. These grids of images relate with each other through commonalities and shifts in their points of view, form, or subject. If, for example, the preacher is searching for images appropriate to a move dealing with Israel's triumphalist self-understanding, within a sermon on the parable of the mustard seed, the image of the cedar of Lebanon is already given in the Psalms and Ezekiel. An adjacent move which focuses on our images of power and glory might interact by an association of form and point of view (space shuttle, Washington monument, big-steeple church). The caution here is that such associations and shifts within image systems should never be made blatantly or self-consciously. Done effectively, however, "they function powerfully because they function subliminally" *(PM)*. It is important to note, Buttrick cautions, that these image grids tie together only as they relate to the structure of the sermon. In this respect, they must assist the movement and formation of the sermon in consciousness and not use their power to detract from or alter the sermon's structural intention.

Analyzing how a homiletic which involves a structural analysis of Scripture and a phenomenology of human consciousness works is at least a distinctive challenge. The method may be understood best by aligning Buttrick's approach to the specifics of sermon preparation with a finished product—his sermon on Abraham and Isaac (pp. 166-69). The intention, then, is to see the movement from text to sermon as well as an actual sermon shaped according to this method.

1. Structure and movement. Having examined the movement and performative intention of the language of the text (in this case, Gen. 22:1-4 and secondarily, Rev. 5:11-14), the structure of the pericope is identified as a sequence of episodes. Homiletically, the challenge now is to develop a series of moves which will express the "logic" of the text. In the sermon on Abraham and Isaac, the following moves can be readily spotted:

a. For Abraham, everything is riding on Isaac.
b. But God's command to Abraham is to kill his only child.
c. Incredibly, Abraham obeys God.
d. But God lovingly provides a lamb to sacrifice.
e. In place of blind obedience, God set Abraham free for faith.
f. So we, too, are free, to trust God and let go.

Having now established the moves and their sequence in the sermon, the next hurdle for the preacher is to probe what is theologically at stake within each of the moves *(FSH)*. While a topic should not be objectified out of the text, it is both appropriate and necessary to explore thoroughly what each move implies as it functions within a theological field of concern. It is quite evident from this sermon, for example, that Buttrick wants to convey the radical character of the command of God that Isaac be killed. Rather than beginning the sermon with the command, the first move underlines for the hearers how much was "wrapped up" in Isaac. Not just an *only child,* but the promise of God itself and the blessing given Abraham and Sarah in Isaac are at stake.

What is also evident is that Buttrick wants to overcome the then-now dichotomy early in the sermon; the ways in which we, too, tend to view everything as wrapped up in one overriding value is established. As the theological implications of the moves are elaborated, the "logic" of the sermon's structure and movement becomes evident. The God who in the second move wants to take away "all our loves" now appears in move four as one who gives all love by handing over an only child. Structurally, reversal is built into the sermon at two levels—one of Divine command and self-giving and the other expressing our human temptation to cling to absolutes. "Everything we got is wrapped up in you" as opposed to the word of grace, "Let go, trust God." This chiastic movement of sermonic structure becomes evident only as the theological significance of each move is expanded. In fact, Buttrick notes, "the odd idea that preachers can move from text to sermon without recourse to theology by some exegetical magic or a leap of homiletic imagination is obvious nonsense" (*IP,* p. 57).

> **2. *Identifying the "contrapuntal."*** Once the sermon's movement and structure have been shaped and each respective move has been theologically explored, it is tempting to want to begin developing systems of illustration. An important intervening step for Buttrick is to question each move with regard to the resistance it will evoke in the listeners. What are the factors which will make it difficult for a congregation to hear this move? *(FTS)* These obstacles are crucial to identify for a homiletic method which depends on a mobile sequence of thoughts forming in consciousness. If one point of a conceptual sermon fails to communicate because of a resistance to the message, there are always the other points. But in a method where the sermon's logic is

embodied within a sequence of movements in group consciousness, the loss of any move will probably be disastrous. Therefore, each move will be queried as to points of likely resistance and strategies will be devised to overcome or bypass the blocks. As the "Abraham and Isaac" moves are reviewed for contrapuntal possibilities, the way in which Buttrick develops the second move suggests that he has realized the need to deal with pietism's romantic notions of prayer and religiosity. It is inescapable, by the time the move has concluded, that God has said to Abraham, "Kill him off!"

3. Imaging the move. Once the moves of the sermon are established and theologically expanded, and once the contrapuntal elements are located, the preacher is now confronted with the challenge of providing imagery for each move. "In preaching," Buttrick insists, "every idea must be imagined and, if possible, connected to actualities in human experience" (*PCF,* p. 52). There is the need then, for each move to be imaged out of the lived experience of the congregation, for without such "fleshing out" the ideas will be "merely heard as words in speech" (*PCF,* p. 52). In order for a move to form in consciousness, it must be imaged for the hearers. "Groups will never trouble to image an abstract word (e.g., clarity, relationships, material things, joys, or sorrows)" (*PCF,* p. 52).

The search for images, of course, begins with the interpretation of Scripture. Not only is the shape and intention of the pericope of central importance, but its imagery as well. In the course of sermon preparation, though, Buttrick encourages a free hand in creating or identifying images which may *possibly* find their way into the sermon itself. Later in the process, many of the potential choices will need to be rejected as not in harmony with the theology of the move or for a number of other reasons.[15] But initially, it is important to allow the imagination to range widely in search of images which might relate to the move's conceptual structure. Turning to the images Buttrick selected for his Abraham-Isaac sermon, we can easily identify the following:

Move I: Little story of the American playwrights-
           Jewish parents—"Everything we got's
           wrapped up in you."

Move II: Contrasting images of our comfortable
           therapist's office with a couch called "Prayer"
           and the text's images of "a stony place, a
           funeral pyre, and a knife blade flashing."
           Image system is completed with quote from
           British novel, "All our loves you take away."

Move III: Contrasting images of our easy-going ap-
           proach to religion ("you can talk religion
           down at the University Club") and a strange
           kind of fanatic obedience ("Abraham pass-
           ing out the poisoned Kool-Aid," the Peni-
           tentes tribe).

Move IV: Byzantine wall-painting of the crucified
           Lamb.

Move V: God's gifts turned into idols: Bible ("we flank
           the open page with candles"), masculine
           church ("protecting the pronouns"), liturgy
           (Catholic journal reader's response to ver-
           nacular Mass).

Move VI: Minister who papered her study walls with
           message, "Trust God, let go."

What is demonstrated here, as Buttrick has argued, is that
the images not only concretely express the theology of the
move, but interact with one another in a gridded system.
Thus, the quotation, "Everything we got's wrapped up in
you," functions variously as Abraham's dilemma (Move I),
our idolatry (Move V), and God's self-giving (Move IV). The
critically important image in the introduction, the medieval
painting of the sacrifice of Isaac, is intended to interlock in
consciousness with the Byzantine painting of the crucified
Lamb. Contrasting images are employed chiefly within a
specific move (II and III), although the quotation in Move II,

"All our loves you have taken away," is reversed in Move IV as God gives an only Child.

What is not provided at any point in the sermon is illustrative material which only ornaments a proposition and is therefore dispensable. The formation of each move in the group consciousness comes through the interplay of conceptual material and imagery. The latter do not illustrate, but contribute to the meaning at stake. Moreover, when viewed as an interlocking grid, none of Buttrick's images can be simply deleted without seriously affecting the logic and movement of the sermon.

4. *Perspectuality and point of view.* David Buttrick makes a distinction between perspectuality and point of view, although at first glance they may be taken for the same homiletic quality. The latter element, point of view, pertains specifically to images and relates to their angle of vision within consciousness. In many cases, point of view is so inherently linked to an image that it is usually conveyed without special attention—"Watching the evening news, we saw . . ."; "Entering town, you pass by an old road sign which announces. . . ." When point of view is not so immediately given, Buttrick encourages the preacher to assist the congregation in experiencing the image by providing such focus or perspective.[16] Two strong words of caution, however, are repeatedly issued concerning misuse of point of view. First, he advises that the images *all* be focused from the point of view of the congregation, never the preacher. Such a first person point of view from the pulpit inevitably splits the focus of the congregation; they are asked to attend to the preacher and an image at the same time. Second, uncontrolled shifts in point of view will also create a split in focus in the congregation's consciousness. Most frequently, these occur as temporal shifts (entering the biblical world as "then" and "now" interchangeably) or narrative shifts (asking the congregation to hear a story from third person and then from first person without relocating its focus). In any case, loss of control is disastrous; "if you shift point-of-view and you don't know it, your congregation freaks right out" *(FTS)*.

The question of perspectuality operates at a more fundamental level within Buttrick's phenomenological method. While point of view relates specifically to an image's angle of vision, the perspectual angle refers to the orientation of the move itself within consciousness. "Each move comes from a different perspectual angle" *(FTS)*, and thereby functions hermeneutically. Through the sequence of moves, therefore, the preacher will be shifting perspectuality as the sermon travels through consciousness, with an attendant "awesome power." Resorting to imagery, Buttrick likens the preacher's control over perspectuality to a spotlight playing on an otherwise darkened stage. Movement is sustained as now this and now that scene is illuminated *(FTS)*. Within the Abraham-Isaac sermon, each move is shaped with reference to some perspectual angle. The first move displays a somewhat complex perspectuality; rather than focusing on the past (through some narrative point of view, for example), the hearer is asked to *remember* the story while looking forward to the promise. The "Jewish parents" quotation does not alter this perspective, but reinforces it. In Move II, an initial perspective ("on a couch called 'Prayer' ") is evoked and quickly quashed by the images of sacrifice and the "All our loves . . ." statement. The third move lacks a strong perspectuality, perhaps because it is trying to deal with Abraham's fanatic obedience and our lukewarm liberal stance. However, a strong sense of perspectuality is reintroduced in Move IV through the focus on the crucified Lamb. In the fifth move, the perspective assumes the hearers to be low-grade idolaters of some sort or another, while the last move identifies the congregation with the minister viewing the Good News covering her office walls. What becomes evident is that perspectuality is as much a designed-in aspect of the sermon as the moves or images themselves. In no case is a perspectual angle repeated, nor the control over perspectuality lost, as the sermon shifts the hearers within hermeneutic consciousness *(FTS)*.

5. Introductions and conclusions. A sermon introduction in David Buttrick's method must be precisely designed in accordance with its homiletic function. Prior to an analysis of these "design specifications," it is important to note what the introduction does *not* have as its purposes within a phenomenlogical method. First, since there is a confidence that an episodic structure of well-designed moves will retain congregational attention, the conceptual sermon's "arouse high interest" approach is unneeded *(FSH)*. The idea that an introduction should through its winsome anecdotes and humor attempt to carry congregational attention well into a topical sermon is now obsolete. Second, the romantic notion that the introduction is the occasion for a preacher's self-disclosure is likewise rendered null and void by Buttrick's method. Whether in an introduction or elsewhere in the sermon, first person stories from the pulpit inevitably evoke a confusion of focus. "We cannot prevent them from splitting; that is, a story meant to illustrate *X* will wind up illustrating you" *(PM)*. Finally, a sermon introduction is not an occasion for a display of the preacher's exegetical expertise. Such "talk about" Scripture is both self-serving (it draws attention to the preacher) and detrimental to the intention of the sermon.

The nature of a sermon introduction, then, will be reformed according to its quite specific functions within the overall homiletic intention of the sermon. Most importantly, an introduction will function hermeneutically to orient the listeners to the text from some particular stance. For example, Buttrick has used the introduction to "Abraham and Isaac" to establish an image of the sacrifice of Isaac which will remain a paradigm throughout the sermon. However, he also removes the issue from the "History of Religions School" ("What can we make of that ancient Hebraic story?") and contemporizes it for us ("from Augustine to Kafka, from Kierkegaard to Karl Barth"). As a sort of by-product of this primary hermeneutic function, a sermon introduction should also be designed to gather congregational attention and provide a readiness to hear the first move. People who prior to the introduction have their attention divided a hundred ways—from a concern over the preacher's uneven stole to the roast in the oven—are all provided one focus (the image of Isaac's sacrifice) and one question ("What can we make of the story?").

Given these performative goals, a sermon introduction will gain several concrete design specifications. "You cannot do an introduction in less than seven sentences," Buttrick states, "and you cannot use more than twelve" *(FTS)*. Less than seven sentences will not provide enough speech for the congregation to "tune in" to the preacher while "after twelve people get very restive" *(FTS)*. The language of an introduction, moreover, should be relatively simple—complex sentence structure is especially to be avoided here. Also, the preacher should avoid any internal enumeration, "points," or other complexity of organization within the introduction. The hermeneutic function, which is central, is mostly thwarted by such tactics. Rather, through simple sentences with highly "vernacular" language, the congregation is brought to focus at the threshold of the first move *(IS)*. In some instances, Buttrick notes a special hermeneutic function will be added to those already explored. This occurs when the congregation owns a prior understanding of the text which will obstruct their fresh hearing of its intention. So, a sermon on Luke 15:1-8 might need to be introduced by asking: "Which one of you, if you had a hundred sheep out in the wilderness, and if you lost one of those sheep, would leave the ninety-nine and seek out the one that was lost? And the answer is, none of you would!" *(IS)* Here, the preacher must do some ground-clearing on our romanticizing of all the "good shepherds" in first-century Palestine before the radical action of the parable's shepherd can be heard.

The sermon conclusion will share some of the characteristics of the introduction, according to Buttrick. Simplicity of language and absence of complex interval structure will mark conclusions, which are restricted in length to about five to seven sentences *(IS)*. And whatever else, sermon conclusions must not "conclude" in the sense expressed in the traditional conceptual understanding. That is, since the purpose of the sermon is not to marshall evidence to support a thesis or main idea, the conclusion will not be an occasion of summary and "QED." In fact, Buttrick observes, conclusions which tie down and strongly package a sermon's message tend to work against any congregational appropriation. When sermons over-conclude, the tendency is for the hearers to relax and to distance themselves from the implications *(IS).* Rather, the appropriate tenor of a sermon conclusion is less dogmatic and more evocative, leaving matters somewhat open and unresolved. Especially in the case where the pericope contains a tensive or evocative sense of an ending, the sermon is called to do the same. The "conclusion" for such texts will of necessity be in the week-in, week-out, lived experience of the hearers.

6. Move design. In contrast to the wide variety of perspectual angles and the mobility of structure made possible through a sequence of sermonic moves, the internal design of any move will conform to several basic norms. The goal, of course, is that the move will form within group consciousness, yet come to some closure at its end in order that the sermon's episodic movement may continue. First of all, then, the language at the beginning and end of a move will need to function quite specifically in relationship to the theological intent of the move. A "conceptual" needs to be established, Buttrick indicates, which will serve as an ideational setting within which the move will happen *(FTS).* In order to create this conceptual, relatively simple sentences need to indicate what the move is about but without introducing much information at first. In other words, the first two or three sentences of a move will serve to express the conceptual by a kind of intentional reiteration. This principle is clearly observable in Buttrick's language in "Abraham and Isaac" as it opens each move:

a. "At the outset, notice: Isaac is much more than an only child. *Isaac is hope,* hope wrapped up in human flesh. All the promises of God were riding on Isaac."

c. "Then, of all things, *Abraham obeyed.* Abraham did as he was told. He obeyed. Flat-eyed, grim, Abraham led his son up the hill, muttering 'God will provide,' 'God will provide,' with biting irony."

Part of the reasoning behind this reiterative introduction is that persons in groups (congregations, for example) no longer hear the first sentence of a unit of meaning in oral communication. "Oral language forms differently in the group mind than in one-to-one," Buttrick notes *(FTS)*. While the latter forms more rapidly, it does not deal on as many levels at once. Oral language in groups takes longer to form, but can express many more levels of meaning at once *(FTS)*. The implication for move design is seen in the language of the Abraham-Isaac sermon. Each move is established initially in the group consciousness by a series of two or three sentences which focus the conceptual.

As regards endings, one of Buttrick's chief criticisms of topical preaching is that it exhibits no closure system. The group mind will not cease thinking about a point simply by the enumeration of the next point, nor does a "transition" provide for such closure *(IS)*. Actually, transitions, if they work at all, will be taken as additional points, adding to the congregation's confusion as to their location in the sermon. Yet some sense of closure is needed in order to stop the functioning of a move in consciousness and to thereby provide readiness for a new conceptual to be established. The simplest approach, for Buttrick, is some sort of reiteration of the opening conceptual material. Thus Move I of his sermon ends much the same way as it began. "Listen, Isaac was more than an only child. Isaac embodied the promises of God. 'Everything we got is wrapped up in you, boy.' Isaac was hope, all the hope in the world." If the opening and closing of a move establish its conceptual meaning much as a frame surrounds a painting, its internal form is a designed interweaving of conceptual material and imagery. Here, Buttrick offers the following guidelines for developing the internal form of a move:

A. Provide no more than three or four sentences of conceptual material before pausing to image in some way. Unrelieved conceptual discourse will cease to function in the consciousness of groups quite rapidly *(IS)*.

B. The maximum number of internal parts to a move is limited to three; "no human mind will accept more than three internal parts for a single idea" *(FTS)*.

C. Each move will need to be designed with a different internal organization *(FTS)*. Retention drops rapidly if the hearers experience repeated patterns—as in the usual illustrative material of topical preaching.

D. "Each move comes from a different perspectual angle" *(FTS)*. Conceptual preaching's unrelieved third person perspective is deadening to "an attendant consciousness."

E. "Each move is built out of communal language. . . . One-to-one language won't be heard" *(FTS)*.

F. In developing an image within a move, if more than one sentence is employed, the preacher probably should use no more than three" *(PM)*. For a story illustration, the maximum length is five sentences *(PM)*.

G. Conventional illustrative material such as long quotes, poetry, and hymn texts no longer work. A segment of a poem may function, but only if it is contemporary or colloquial *(PM)*.

H. Doublets, paired systems of structure or illustration, do not form in consciousness (two adjacent story illustrations, for example). The group consciousness is not able to handle two elements of equal value at the same time. Typically, one will either dissolve into the other or simply not form at all.[17]

I. In close conjunction, four ideas presented rapidly are almost impossible to hold in consciousness ("The Apostle Paul speaks to us of love, sin, hope, and grace"). Here, the whole system of language tends to collapse in consciousness *(IS)*.

J. The relative strength of imagery and other illustrations needs to be matched with the strength of the move. "The larger the illustration," though, "the more it disconnects from the conceptual" *(PM)*.

7. Stories in preaching. The parameters for story within a phenomenological method have, for the most part, already been given within the discussions of introductions and conclusions, move formation, and point of view. A story could be appropriate within an introduction, providing it served the purpose needed and conformed to the limitations on the number of overall sentences. However, the even more terse requirements of the conclusion would seem to preclude the use of story there, in spite of the current trend of ending a conceptual sermon with a clinching story rather than a poem. Point of view establishes further constraints upon the use of story in Buttrick's method. First person stories by the preacher split congregational focus and, if powerful, blow away the surrounding sermonic material *(IPS)*. The chief problem with a large story within a sermon is that "people get in a story like they get in a 'world' " *(PM)*. The bigger or more powerful the story, the more difficult it is for hearers to extricate themselves and tune back into the sermon's movement and structure. Another current tendency in preaching style, the linking of several stories in succession, is also problematic. Buttrick observes, "If there is no conceptual strength the stories will fight against each other" *(PM)*.

A similar kind of internarrative conflict will occur if too many stories are employed. Of course, these problems will not beset the preacher who utilizes story effectively within the methodological constraints already stated. Story illustrations will work as they concretize the conceptual aspects of the respective moves. However, as can be noted by a review of the Abraham-Isaac sermon, most image systems for David Buttrick do not get elaborated into a full narrative form.

One situation whereby story can expand to become the entire sermon *is* allowed. There are cases where a story can be told by the preacher which with integrity reflects the logic and theological field of concern of a biblical passage. The crafting of a story sermon which will perform with the same intentionality as the pericope is an incredibly difficult challenge. A short-story writer might labor on an analogous work for almost a year. At any rate, Buttrick concludes that a one-story sermon "is so technical a preacher may not be able to design a story well enough" *(PM)*.

If the phenomenological method seems to play out its specific implications in ways that seem overly constraining to the preacher, David Buttrick would probably respond by saying "You betcha you're constrained!" A biblical sermon will be constrained by the scope of a text's structural logic and performative intention. Such preaching is also constrained by the nature of human consciousness today and by the need for a sermon to form in the human mind. Faith does come by hearing, he would remind us. But there is another side to the argument, Buttrick insists, for what is offered is "a whole new way of preaching which does not nail you down, but sets you free to preach the Word of the Lord, which is after all, what preaching is all about" *(FSH)*. What seems like undue restraints, it is argued, actually provide for a liberating of the awesome power of preaching. So he concludes:

> When a new homiletic, tuned to hermeneutic sensitivity and a tough phenomenological analysis of language, emerges and filters down to the pastor's study, we may see a generation of preachers who find Scripture exciting and who find speaking in grace an act of radical obedience *(IP,* p. 58).

Evaluation

Any evaluation of the homiletics of David Buttrick must begin with an acknowledgment of the distinctiveness of his approach. His "phenomenological method" is in many regards unique among the viable methods of biblical preaching today. While speaking of Scripture and preaching as plotted systems of language, he is not dependent on the primacy of narrative as *the* hermeneutical principle. And while he insists that both the scriptural pericope and the sermon are moving plots exhibiting some "theo-logic," there is no assumption as to a normative sermonic movement such as is seen in an inductive homiletics. Indeed, the most distinctive characteristic of Buttrick's method is his refusal to impose any prior structural restraint on the form and movement of the sermon. Only the biblical passage itself can disclose the road map for the preacher as to the shape and mobility of the sermon.

What Buttrick does hold in common with his "new hearing" colleagues, of course, is a strong solidarity regarding the whole project of the old, conceptual homiletics. The obsolescence and deadliness of discursive preaching derive from its misuse of Scripture through the application of its method of distillation. Burdened with a rationalist bias, the old homiletic is based on a static model of argumentation derived from Hellenistic rhetoric. The result of this aggregate of ideas and propositions is a static system which addresses only the cognitive aspects of human personality. But while agreeing with Rice, Mitchell, Lowry, and Craddock on these points of criticism, Buttrick adds one final, decisive critique. Conceptual preaching is not only dated when viewed from the perspectives of the new biblical studies and hermeneutic theory, it plainly does not function any longer as effective proclamation of the gospel. If faith comes from hearing, topical preaching is in trouble because it is no longer heard by the congregation.

Beyond this solidarity with the narrative and inductive homileticians as regards the inadequacies of discursive preaching, the phenomenological method involves some unique assets as well as problems, particularly when it is commended as the ongoing approach to the preaching task. Among the strengths of this approach, the following should certainly be taken into account by any prospective "patch-work phenomenologist":

1. Buttrick's analysis of the factors involved in the linguistic crisis seems unarguable. Language is experiencing rapid quantitative and qualitative change in Western culture, and these massive changes point to severe shifts and dislocations in social consciousness. Preaching clearly cannot act as if this revolution in language and culture is not drastically affecting its capability to communicate. However, the way out, Buttrick suggests, is precisely given in a recovery of the performative capacities of biblical language. There is a potency and intentionality to the language of Scripture, and

the preacher is asked to be keenly attentive to this "doing" of the text as well as its meaning. Drawing on the insights of literary-critical scholarship, Buttrick approaches the pericope seeking its intention as expressed within the performance of its language.

2. Closely associated with this accuracy of assessment regarding language's impoverishment and potency is Buttrick's keen insight into the state of what he calls "hermeneutic consciousness." The insistence that the sermon must form in group consciousness much as thoughts form in the mind involves the preacher in considerations of perspectuality, image systems, and most importantly, the identification of the "move" as the basic component of sermonic structure. Again, Buttrick's argument is compelling. If, in fact, meaning is discovered in phenomenal consciousness to be sequentially ordered systems of language utilizing both conceptual material and images, then the sermon will need to pattern itself after this system if it is to form within the group consciousness of the congregation. To see a sermon as a plotted system of language moving through some theological field, forming in consciousness as it moves, is to acquire a new way of preaching. The break with the old homiletic orthodoxy is complete, since this phenomenological kind of preaching, with its emphasis on mobile structures of meaning, can never be reduced to a thematic distillate. On the other hand, when preaching does form in consciousness and move with the intention of the text, the outcome, as Buttrick would put it, is "awesome."

3. On the basis of the first two values within the approach of David Buttrick, a third may be noted. Whereas Fred Craddock insists on a discontinuity between exegetical and homiletic method, the phenomenological method unites them in common attention to the performative intention of both text and sermon. Without slavishly imitating the structure of the pericope, the sermon will need to be designed to function in the consciousness of its hearers much as the text functioned for its hearers. The sermon will

replicate the "logic" of the text by a similar movement through the same theological field. For Buttrick's method, then, the same interpretive skills which are needed to detect the structure and movement of the text will be of immediate significance for creating a sermon which will reflect the same intentionality. To become this sort of "homiletical exegete" is to discover a way out of the impasse created by the tendency of historical-critical interpretation to distance the text from the world of the preacher and hearers.

4. While David Buttrick shares with narrative and inductive homileticians an appreciation of language that is concrete and filled with imagery, only he has explored the more formal characteristics of imagery from a hermeneutical perspective. The value of imagery for preaching is acknowledged by all of the homileticians under consideration here. What Buttrick adds is a hermeneutical foundation which establishes the essential role of image within a plotted system of oral address. Lacking the immediacy of image, language is no longer heard, nor does it now form as thought. Based on this hermeneutic significance of imagery, Buttrick is then able to move effectively to such issues of homiletic praxis as point of view, image systems within moves, and the interaction of images throughout the sermon. In this regard, a whole new arena of exploration has been opened within homiletic theory and practice. Learning why one should image a sermon and *how* to image it will be important considerations for a whole new generation of ministers seeking to preach biblically.

The difficulties of this phenomenological method are best detected by considering it from the perspective of a preacher who is interested in trying it out. That is, the success of this distinctive approach to preaching largely depends on the degree to which it is comprehensible and adaptable for the preacher who is a novice to the system. Assuming that she or he is convinced of Buttrick's analysis of the pathology of the old preaching, and is mostly won over to a literary-critical approach to biblical interpretation, what problems are likely to be encountered as sermons are developed according to the Buttrick method?

The first problem to confront the budding "patchwork phenomenologist" will probably relate to the task of scriptural analysis. Armed chiefly with historical-critical training, a preacher new to this method will initially have difficulty in identifying a text's internal structure and movement. This first stage of interpretation, involving a surface-level structural analysis of the pericope, is essential to the whole project, yet at present there is minimal interpretive assistance at hand. Most popular-level commentaries will be of no help whatsoever here, and even the literary-critical investigators are not of a single mind as to the conventions for such structural analysis.[18] And if the novice phenomenological preacher should stumble into the research of the structuralists, the incredibly technical discussions of actants, deixis, and isotopy will probably more befuddle than illuminate.[19] Clearly, Buttrick himself will need to provide the "learner's manual" on this essential task of educing the structural form and movement by which a text's "logic" is evidenced. Assistance is especially needed in plotting the logic of non-narrative biblical material and those pericopes whose full structural logic involves moves which are only implied.

A second major challenge which confronts the preacher undertaking the phenomenological approach is the formation of that basic module of meaning within the sermonic structure, the move. Even if the basic directions have been assimilated ahead of time, the technical issues of opening and closure systems, interaction of conceptual material and imagery, and perspectuality may seem overwhelming to the novice. The specifications for move formation appear both too simple and too complex at the same time—too simple with respect to certain parameters and too complex because the same parameters allow for such a diversity of choices. For example, when Buttrick insists that perspectuality be taken into account as a dimension of the meaning of a move, the alternatives at first seem quite obvious—"then or now," "pulpit perspective or people perspective," "we" or "they."

Yet in one sermon on Mark 2:15-17, Buttrick developed five consecutive moves, each one focusing the congregation on Jesus' table fellowship with sinners from a different perspective *(FTS)*. Clearly the possibilities, informed by the logic of the text, are remarkably broad for any sequence of moves in a sermon. On the other hand, the technical aspects which make for perspectuality are both precise and delimited. Once more, the need for a handbook on phenomenological preaching is indicated, with an extensive section on move formation and perspectuality, and point of view.

The third area critical to the success of the Buttrick method is that of the imagery within the context of each move. It is repeatedly noted that no more than three or four conceptual sentences can be given during the course of a move without their meaning being imaged. Further employment of conceptual discourse beyond this boundary will seriously jeopardize the retention of the significance of the entire move. The theory here may be clear and certainly resonates with the common sense intuition to be concrete when communicating. In practice, however, what often results as preachers attempt to follow Buttrick's instructions at this point is a rather general "speaking about" rather than a "speaking of" the images. Trained theologically to be articulate, many preachers become stymied when called upon to image in concrete and immediate terms what they can talk about at great length. Some preachers may be able to recall a story which illustrates the conceptual and others may be able to "get in touch with their own feelings" in regard to the conceptual's implications, but the ability to provide images reflecting meaning is an unlearned skill. Here something more than a handbook is needed, involving, perhaps, printing or videotaping a series of sermons in which image has replaced illustration. But best of all may be the homiletic risk which lets go of the old "I've got a story about . . ." type of illustrating in favor of attempts at visually, aurally, or kinesthetically concrete and immediate imaging. Buttrick then asks the hearers following the sermon: "What formed? What did you hear?"

Finally, a concern has been raised at a more formal level. To the extent that this method assumes that the sermon derives its logic and mobility from a biblical passage, a certain portion of Scripture would appear to be unpreachable by virtue of the absence of such logic and mobility. David Buttrick has acknowledged this by admitting that the Psalms and other hymnic material in the Bible are not susceptible to homiletic treatment. While this admission does somewhat limit the preacher's "canon," this limitation is based upon an insistence that all preaching become immediately biblical through its faithfulness to the intentionality and logic of a specific passage of Scripture.

ABRAHAM AND ISAAC

David Buttrick

GENESIS 22:1-4

REVELATION 5:11-14

An old German woodcut pictures the sacrifice of Isaac. There is Isaac, all trussed up, lying on a pile of brush; huge, empty-circle eyes staring. Above him stands Abraham, both hands held high, about to plunge the knife. Over to one side, in a bush, stands a white lamb waiting. What a strange story! The story has troubled religious people for centuries, everyone from Augustine to Kafka, from Kierkegaard to Karl Barth. What can we make of the sacrifice of Isaac? Terror and grace. What can we make of the story?

At the outset, notice: Isaac is much more than an only child. *Isaac is hope,* hope wrapped up in human flesh. All the promises of God were riding on Isaac. Remember the story? Remember how God dropped in to tell Sarah and Abraham that their offspring would be many as the sands of the sea, that they would give birth to nations. Well, the old folks giggled, for according to reliable medical advice it's mighty tough to conceive when you're pushing ninety! Then, suddenly, Isaac was born, a miracle child. God did provide! Through Isaac, there *would* be many descendants, a multitude of nations. An American playwright tells of how his Jewish parents scrimped and saved to give him everything. They bought him new clothes three times a year, bundled him off to private schools, paid for his college education. "Everything we got's wrapped up in you, boy!" his mother used to say. "Everything we got is wrapped up in you." How easy it is to focus our hopes. God gives us a land to live in and, before you know it, we're chanting, "Everything we got is wrapped up in you, America!" Or, a church to belong to: "Everything we got is wrapped up in you, Presbyterian Church!" Listen, Isaac was more than an only child. Isaac embodied the promises of God. "Everything we got is wrapped up in you, boy." Isaac was hope, all the hope in the world.

So what happened? *God spoke. "Kill him off," said God,* "Take your only child and kill him!" We hear the words and we're appalled. We've always talked of God as Love, spelled L-O-O-O-V-E, so the hard words shake us. "Kill him off," said God. Suddenly life is not what we thought it was—a comfortable therapist's office where on a couch called "Prayer" we can spill out our souls to some caring Deity. No. Instead we're stuck with a stony place, a funeral pyre, and a knife blade flashing. Yes, God gives good gifts, but God takes away! "All our loves," cries the heroine of a British novel, "All our loves, you take away!" For every brimming child, there does seem to be a knife blade. So maybe as the theologians say we're going to have to "reconstruct our God-concept" to include a few of the darker shades. God may well be terribly good, but notice the adverb "terribly"! God spoke a terrible word to Abraham. As Abraham stood staring at his child Isaac, God said, "Kill him. Kill him off," God spoke.

Then, of all things, *Abraham obeyed.* Abraham did as he was told. He obeyed. Flat-eyed, grim, Abraham led his son up the hill, muttering "God will provide," "God will provide," with biting irony. Fanatic Abraham obeyed. To most of us, religion's rather easy-going, a liberal persuasion, something that's even passable on campus—you can talk religion down at the University Club. Then we flip a page in our Bibles and stumble on wild-eyed Abraham passing out the poisoned Kool-Aid in some stony Jonestown, and we're embarrassed. Down in the Southwest there's a tribe, the Penitentes. Some say they were practicing human sacrifice into the 1950s. Finally, they were investigated. "What kind of people are you to practice human sacrifice?" a prosecutor demanded. To which a tribal leader replied, "You do not take God seriously." Well, maybe we don't. We are moderate people: We calculate our charities, confess our minimal sins, schedule a Minute for Mission on a weekly basis, and run for dear life from anything in excess. But see in Abraham radical, blind obedience. God commanded, and Abraham was bent on doing God's will even if it meant slaughtering his only hope. So, Abraham went up the hill to kill Isaac. God spoke and Abraham obeyed.

Now, hear the clatter of the knife on stone. See Abraham's arms folded down to his side. For *suddenly Abraham caught sight of the trapped lamb:* "God *will* provide," he cried triumphantly, "God will provide!" Well, if you're Christian, you can't help thinking of Calvary, can you? Of another stone hill, and a high cross. One of the earliest pictures of the Crucifixion is a Byzantine wall-painting. The picture shows the stone hill and the wood-stick cross, but instead of hung Jesus, there's a huge, nailed Lamb on the cross-bar. Lamb of God! Look, if God will hand over an only Child sacrificed to our rigid sins, then see, behind the hard hurt surface of life, there's not a holy terror, but love: Love so amazing, so divine, so unutterably intense it will sacrifice itself for us. Lamb on the cross, then Lamb on the Throne! So Abraham caught sight of the trapped lamb and shouted for joy. Clatter of the knife on stone. Fold of the arm. "God will provide," cried Abraham.

Now do you see what the sacrifice of Abraham is all about? *God set Abraham free for faith.* The Bible calls the story a "test" but the word is too tame. On a high stone hill, God set Abraham free, free for faith. Blind obedience was transformed into faith. Oh, how easy it is to pin all our hopes on a means of grace, and forget God, the giver. So subtly we turn God's gifts into idols. God has given us Scriptures, but see how we flank the open page with candles and frame dogma to guarantee infallibility: "Everything we got's wrapped up in you, Bible!" Or, perhaps God draws us into faith through a masculine Church; before you know it we're protecting the pronouns and two-legged tailored vestments: "Everything we got's wrapped up in you," sung by a bass-voiced choir. Back in the sixties, a liberal Catholic journal announced gleefully, "God can get along without the Latin Mass." To which a reader replied: "Maybe God can, but we can't." Is there any idolatry like religious idolatry? No wonder God speaks and shatters our souls: "Kill it off!" God who takes away all our false loves. So on a high hill, God called up Abraham and Isaac, and there—amazing, ruthless grace—God set Abraham free, free for faith.

Well, *here we are stumbling down a stone hill Calvary into the twentieth century.* We are free to trust God, for God will provide.

Oh, we've still got our Bible, our church, our liturgies, but somehow they are different now: the gilded sheen has rubbed off. We can still love our church, our denominations, without having to hold on for dear life, particularly in an age when God may be sweeping away denominations. And, yes, we can love the Scriptures, without having to defend each sacred page, especially now when authority fights are building. We can trust the self-giving God to give us all we'll ever need: "God will provide!" There's a minister in a northern state who has papered a wall of her office, custom made wallpaper repeating words line after line, all over the space. Now she can sit at her desk and read: "Trust God; let go. Trust God; let go." Because we trust God—Lamb on the Throne—we *can* let go of all our loves: Bible, Church, Nation, even Sexuality. We can stumble down from Calvary into a human world, sure of the grace of God.

Now then, here are pictures to put up in your mind. A stone hill, a pile of brush, empty-circle eyes, and a knife blade high. "Kill him off," cracks the voice of God. But, here's another picture: A wood cross on a rock hill, and a lamb nailed to the cross-bar, "God will provide." Keep *both* pictures in your mind. "You God, you take away all our loves, but you give yourself!" Trust God, let go. Let go, trust God.

NOTES

1. David G. Buttrick, "Preaching the Christian Faith," *Liturgy* 2, no. 3, p. 54. (Hereafter *PCF*.)

2. David G. Buttrick, "Interpretation and Preaching," *Interpretation* 25, no. 1 (Jan. 1981), p. 46. (Hereafter *IP*.)

3. David G. Buttrick, "First Steps for a New Homiletic" (Videotape produced by Board of Discipleship, The United Methodist Church, for use at national preaching event, "Proclamation," Nashville, Tennessee, July 1983). (Hereafter *FSH*.)

4. *IP*, p. 46. Buttrick notes that commentaries have perpetuated a hermeneutic of distillation. Historical-critical scholarship, in its quest for what a text "meant," also tends to treat Scripture as a static system from which concepts are drawn. The result is that students "drift out of seminaries trained in historical-critical method, practiced in homiletic technique, yet at a loss to preach 'biblically.' "

5. David G. Buttrick, "On Liturgical Language," *Reformed Liturgy Music* 15, no. 2 (Spring 1981), p. 74.

6. David Buttrick, "Intensive Seminar on Biblical Preaching" (Sponsored by Board of Discipleship, The United Methodist Church, Nashville, Tennessee, March 1981). (Hereafter *IS*.)

7. Buttrick, "On Liturgical Language," p. 74.

8. David G. Buttrick, "The Powers That Be, Revisited" (Paper delivered at the Hickman Lectures, Duke University Divinity School Convocation, Durham, North Carolina, October 23, 1979).

9. Ibid.

10. Ibid.

11. David G. Buttrick, "From Text to Sermon" (Lecture given at Duke University Divinity School, Durham, North Carolina, April 1984). (Hereafter *FTS*.)

12. *FTS*. Buttrick also observes in this lecture that a "mobile system also works better with women's minds than with men's."

13. David G. Buttrick, "A Phenomenological Method" (Videotape interview at Duke University Divinity School, Durham, North Carolina, April 1984.) (Hereafter *PM*.)

14. In a sermon on Mark 4:1-9, Buttrick images the world rejecting the gospel through an apartment scene from a Broadway play. There is a sophisticated young couple on stage, and through the open apartment window a Salvation Army band is heard playing a gospel song. The husband moves to the window and slams it shut while exclaiming, "Honestly, dear, I do not see what Jesus has to do with us!"

15. See pages 156-57 for Buttrick's approach to the internal organization of a "movement."

16. Interestingly, explicit attention is not devoted to point of view in Buttrick's "Abraham and Isaac" with the exception of the viewers' perspective on the two paintings. Perspectuality, on the other hand, is much more extensively and subtly developed.

17. *IS*. In a later conversation with this author in the fall of 1983, Buttrick indicated that some sequential movement can save two adjacent illustrative systems from becoming doublets. So, an approach which first looks inside

ourselves to see darkness, for example, and then turns in focus to view darkness in the world, will form and thereby avoid the doublet problem.
18. The investigations of the narrative character of the parables by Bernard Brandon Scott in *Jesus, Symbol-Maker for the Kingdom* (Philadelphia: Fortress Press, 1981), pp. 23-58, may be the sort of structural analysis most immediately applicable to Buttrick's phenomenological method. With regard to point of view and perspectuality, R. Alan Culpepper's work, *Anatomy of the Fourth Gospel: A Study in Literary Design* (Philadelphia: Fortress Press, 1983) may be similarly applicable to the Buttrick method.
19. See Daniel Patte, *What is Structural Exegesis?* ed. Dan O. Via, Jr. (Philadelphia: Fortress Press, 1976) for both an introduction to structuralism and an annotated bibliography on structuralist research. Readers are referred to Appendix I in Dan Otto Via's *The Ethics of Mark's Gospel—In the Middle of Time* (Philadelphia: Fortress Press, 1985) for an insightful discussion of the relationship of structuralism and phenomenological hermeneutics. To the extent that "structuralism relates the text to an underlying system of abstractions, while hermeneutics relates it to the reader-interpreter in his life-world" (p. 204), the latter will be of much more immediate significance for preaching and homiletic method than the former.

6

POSTSCRIPT

Story and Storytelling

The ascendance of a homiletics of story is neither an isolated phenomenon within the church today nor without hermeneutical roots shared across a wide range of theological disciplines. This welcome reemergence of the church's narrative self-understanding has been long in coming, but its advent may signal that the conceptual, rationalist bias which has held sway since the Enlightenment is finally beginning to ebb. In its place, the dynamism of the "narrative theology" movement is being felt in almost every corner of the church. With ideological roots in the inquiries of literary criticism and the philosophy of language, the movement may have its Magna Carta in Stephen Crites' seminal paper, "The Narrative Quality of Experience."[1] During the fifteen years since the publication of Crites' work, a considerable variety of narrative theologies have emerged, including a vigorous sub-species of "metaphorical" theologies.[2] It was not until the advent of Michael Goldberg's *Theology and Narrative*,[3] though, that the narrative theology movement achieved a self-critical maturity. After an analysis of the liabilities afflicting those modern systems in theology and ethics which abandoned narrative, Goldberg turned to an exploration of the conditions needed in order for narrative theology to remain of consequence in the religious community. Meanwhile,

Deneise Deter-Rankin is Chaplain to the College and a member of the religion faculty at Queens College, Charlotte, North Carolina.

John Vannorsdall is President of the Lutheran Theological Seminary at Philadelphia, Philadelphia, Pennsylvania.

closely related developments in the fields of ethics (James McClendon and Stanley Hauerwas) and Christian education (Jerome Berryman and John Westerhoff) also have manifested refreshing new approaches based on the interpretive model of story.[4]

At the heart of this widespread interest in narrative, of course, is a new probing by biblical scholars into the nature of Scripture as story.[5] Studies in the parables, to take a notable example, have exhibited an explosive new vigor during this same period.[6] With both theology and biblical interpretation moving beyond the restrictions of former rationalist assumptions, it was inevitable that the field of homiletics, too, would find itself called to renewal. The overriding reason, however, for a return to an insistence on preaching the story is Goldberg's insight that biblical narratives "reflect the primary structure of existence, make basic claims about the truth of that existence, and display the ways whereby such existence may be fundamentally affected and transformed."[7] The recovery of narrative in both interpretation and homiletic method, then, has proven of major significance to the revival of an almost dormant field of homiletics as well as a renewal of the likewise dormant pulpit.

To locate preaching as storytelling within the more comprehensive context of narrative hermeneutics and theology is not to be understood as endorsing the new status quo in preaching. Preaching as story is likely to become yet another fad in the church's life unless several problematic issues are addressed at the levels of both homiletical theory and praxis.

The most obvious issue is that a great number of sermons week in and week out continue to manifest a misuse of story and of storytelling. Mostly this misuse relates to the utilization of story as illustration, decoration, and embellishment of an essentially topical sermon. Employing a homiletics of distillation, it is assumed that biblical narrative can be rendered into some point or other, which can then be "illustrated" by other stories. Moreover, in these latter days of topical preaching a trend may be detected for stories to expand to elephantine proportions, especially when they are made to serve as sermon introductions. Such extended story introductions actually function in a quasi-scriptural role, providing whatever thematic control is present within the sermon along with the authoritative warrant for its "proclamation." More often than not these swollen stories are apologue rather than metaphor—they are designed to deliver a message. And predictably, such stories scold, moralize, or are emotionally manipulative, dealing more in law than in gospel. Clearly, these expressions of "storytelling" do not constitute biblical preaching within any of the homiletical options we have examined. The radical character of narrative in Scripture and church tradition is violated regularly by not a few preachers marching under the storytelling banner.

A second issue of serious consequence for preaching today is that those who are leading the preaching-as-storytelling movement have not engaged in adequate dialog with their fellow travelers in related disciplines. For the most part, there has been a persistent delay of over a decade before the research of those engaged in hermeneutics and literary criticism has been incorporated into homiletic method. Perhaps such a frustrating lag is inevitable, but it is to be hoped that more recent scholarship in these seminal fields can be incorporated into homiletical discussions at a more rapid pace. Of greater concern, however, is the tendency of narrative homileticians to work in the field at a surface level of engagement, when compared to their colleagues in theology and ethics. In *Theology and Narrative,* for example, Goldberg justifies a narrative theology only if it meets certain necessary primary conditions:

(1) that what is used as the basis for theological reflection is a narrative and not, e.g., some discursive philosophical system or some randomly selected passages;

(2) that whatever narrative is used has been properly identified and subsequently used as the kind of narrative it is, e.g., a myth and not an historical account; and

(3) that whatever narrative is used has been correctly understood within the context of meaning provided by the communal tradition which claims it as its own.[8]

Our present survey has found in the homileticians operating out of a narrative method a crucial vulnerability to at least one of these criteria. Rice evidences strengths in the first and third of these norms, but lacks precision at the point of clarity of narrative identification, particularly with reference to metaphor. Mitchell shows great awareness of the importance of the communal tradition and is productively engaged at present in exploring the second issue. To the extent that he retains the main idea telos for the sermon and persists in extracting points from the narrative, there is a potential weakness regarding the first of Goldberg's concerns. Yet another violation of this first issue is seen in the persistence of a homiletic of catharsis within Lowry's approach. Put simply, the challenge Michael Goldberg directs at narrative theologians and ethicists is also directed at the narrative homileticians. And for the sake of the future of preaching as storytelling, this more radical engagement concerning the hermeneutics of narrative needs to begin.

Narrative and Image

It should be instructive for homileticians that, as ethicists seek to develop the notion of character within a narrative context, it becomes necessary to explore the significance of *images* in relation to story. The narrative character of the activity of God and human life is essential to ethics, Stanley Hauerwas maintains, because a non-historical, "objective" position for defining a Christian ethic is unavailable. "We are unable to stand outside our histories in mid-air, as it were; we are destined to discover ourselves only within God's history, for God is our beginning and our end."[9] This theological centrality of narrative for Christian life is essential, therefore, because it discloses the contingent and historical nature of human life. An individual's identity and morality are derived from living in a community sustained by a living tradition;

"we discover the self through a community's narrated tradition."[10] Moreover, Hauerwas maintains that this ecclesial and personal identity is given by way of narrative since God's self-revelation occurs through the history of the covenant people and in the life, death, and resurrection of Jesus. Hence, "by learning to be [Jesus'] disciples we will learn to find our life—our story—in God's story."[11]

Given this essential nature of narrative for Christian life and action, the task of ethics within the church is first to call attention not to a corpus of duties, but to a story-formed way of envisioning the world. For Hauerwas, then, "the enterprise of Christian ethics primarily helps us to see. We can only act within the world we can envision, and we can envision the world rightly only as we are trained to see."[12] Not only narratives, but images as well are at the heart of Christian life; envisioning the world depends on both. At this point, Hauerwas reveals his own dependence on Austin Farrer's foundational exploration of the significance of images for revelation and human response.[13] This decisive function of images in envisioning the world is most explicitly developed for theological ethics by James McClendon, who is equally indebted to Farrer. McClendon would agree with his mentor that Christian faith consists "especially in the application to one's own circumstances of appropriate biblical images."[14] He adds: "Christian faith comprises images applied to life, and . . . the understanding of that faith must involve the examination of the role of images in actual lives, the role of images in the experience of life."[15] But neither McClendon nor Hauerwas would posit the adequacy of images alone. They are given within and carried by a narrative-based communal tradition—the story of God's dealing with Israel and with the New Israel in Jesus.

Given this attention to the formative role of images in the determination of Christian community and personal character, it is peculiar that none of the narrative homileticians surveyed have sought to explore the relationship between narrative and image. Only David Buttrick among our homileticians attended to the significance of imagery for preaching, though his method does not assume any normative status for narrative plots as opposed to other scriptural "plots." Therefore, it has not been necessary thus far for him to engage in a systematic analysis of the interaction of image and narrative. Yet such an exploration may be needful for all of those who seek to move beyond the old discursive preaching. And it may well be that the next stages in the development of homiletic method will depend upon these considerations.

When the relationship between narrative and image is explored, the primacy of story seems inescapable. The very medium of language gives to narrative a sense of duration—a quality of direction intrinsic to written or oral language which connotes "the notion of the passage of time."[16] As a function of plot, particularly, "the time of a narrative [is] at least potentially reflective or imitative of the time of human experience generally."[17] The stories of our lives are much like life. There are beginnings and endings, and between, the waiting, the reversals, and the surprises that are the stuff of human existence. But our experience is not always ordered and connected. On the contrary, at its depths life is experienced through inchoate and unstoried images which are nevertheless incredibly powerful in their meaning and affective value.[18] Of course, we typically incorporate these primordial images into some narrative framework or other, or repress them entirely if they do not "fit." If the dissonance becomes too great, it may be time for psychotherapy and/or hypnotism. At any rate, these images do lurk in human subconsciousness and are profoundly determinative of human behavior.[19]

On the other hand, certain stories evoke images which then persist as their own centers of meaning. The cross gains its own life and power from the passion narrative, as do the bread and wine from the various stories of Jesus' meals with his followers. But while such imagery may seem to achieve an independence from its narrative locus, an undue separation of an image from its story involves a threat to both entities. "When images lose their anchorage in stories, they are

177

divested of much of their significance and begin to drift aimlessly, growing enigmatic and increasingly indeterminate."[20] Historians of the liturgy, for example, point to the loss of the eucharistic narrative in Western tradition as creating precisely this crisis for the meaning of the images of bread and wine. Images remain slippery and obscure, until they are located within a narrative. David Harned observed, "To name an image is to furnish it with a context—in other words, to place it within a story."[21]

The relationship of narrative and image, then, is both essential and reciprocal. Narrative provides for a sense of temporal succession, evoking plot and the experience of time. But these qualities of narrative are precisely a disadvantage, as Weismann detects, "when simultaneity of various ideas, events, or opposed qualities is desired."[22] An image therefore offers what narrative cannot achieve—"a single configuration with implicit meaning."[23] The reciprocal character of the relationship between narrative and image is equally significant. Apart from stories, Harned notes, images do not automatically interact with coherent meaning. They are external to each other and "their relationship is not one of simple increment but of tension and conflict."[24] "Only the art of narrative can disclose how different images are intended to be weighed in relation to one another, or which of various subordinate images the crucial ones are meant to include and which they are fashioned to deny."[25] Moreover, an image's narrative context provides for an interpretative decision regarding the multiple meanings inherent in the image.

It is also the case, however, that the image itself may serve as the hermeneutical perspective from which the entire story is received. Within imagery we find the "adumbrations of, clues to, and canons of interpretation for the story itself."[26] Their concreteness and capacity to offer meaning as a *Gestalt* allows a story to be experienced as real, as my story, and potentially, as *the* Story. Images, then, provide a point of view for a story while offering immediately available cognitive and affective significance. The manual act of the breaking of bread evokes the story, while the broken bread as an image serves to interpret both the story and the assembly as well. At this level of significance, images may gain an iconic function, linking the interpreter in communion with the whole subject of the story. "The sacramental power of an icon is its symbolic capacity for *anamnesis;* it is the best available [i.e., symbolic] means for *recalling* or invoking *the true presence* of its subject or prototype."[27] Iconic images, then, we shall designate as those images which provide a holistic perception of a story and invite the hearer/interpreter to fully participate in its meaning and power.[28]

A final characteristic of imagery relates to the quality of experience evoked through the interplay of images within some fields of meaning (though not necessarily a narrative field). Contrary to Harned's insistence, the presence of diversity among images does not always call for a story context to bring unity and specificity. Poetry and liturgical prayer both have the capacity to offer images which creatively interact and thereby disclose their inner reality.[29] Bozarth-Campbell speaks of this transformation as a work of incarnation; the words and the images join in mutual interpretation. "The primary communication between images creates tensiveness as they flow into and move against each other, to progress from visual to auditory to kinesthetic levels."[30] Of course, this interplay of imagery may occur within a narrative context as well, and in fact, the iconic and incarnational efficacy of imagery may best occur within story. Those who do theology, homiletics, or ethics from the perspective of a narrative hermeneutical norm, however, have the burden of establishing the essential primacy of story.

The implications for homiletic method of these explorations of the relationship of narrative and image are clearly provisional at this stage of development. Yet this discussion does serve to confirm David Buttrick's insistence on the need for concrete imagery within each movement of the sermon. Then, too, Buttrick may be invited to explore this iconic quality of image with reference to his treatment of perspectuality and point of view. These iconic images are frequently experienced in the preaching of Fred Craddock, though he has not as yet explored their significance with respect to either inductive or narrative homiletic systems. It is to the narrative homileticians that these questions must be most directly addressed, however, since they have forged rather complete homiletic methods without taking into account the focal significance of image at the hermeneutic stage of their systems. To the extent that their hermeneutics does not take into account narrative *and* image, it would seem that the methodological outcome remains vulnerable and unfulfilled. A deeper hermeneutical plowing may quite possibly produce an even more productive methodological yield for the storytellers.

An Implicit Homiletic?

There may well be another homiletic option which presents itself on the basis of this interaction between narrative and image. Although such a relationship between narrative and image has been explored elsewhere, as we have seen, its specific implications for homiletic method have remained largely unexplored. On the other hand, an increasing number of preachers are developing sermons utilizing both narrative systems and imagery, apart from any formal methodological considerations. Within the scope of this eclectic and, in many cases, intuitively developed corpus of sermons, however, two alternative models of narrative and image interaction can be detected and analyzed as to their respective methods.

The first model is seen most clearly in the preaching of John Vannorsdall as well as in his reflections on his sermons.[31] "An effective story," he observes, "depends upon images made of words spoken one at a time and chosen in such a way that the hearer can receive the words and with the imagination reconstruct an image which is key to the one offered, but distinctly his or her own."[32] As Vannorsdall develops and interprets "The Wilderness and the Dry Land" (pp. 184-85), one of three short sermons presented in his

article "Esthetics and Preaching," this imaginative reconstruction of images is clearly presented.[33]

The overriding image in this sermon is the biblical one of
the wilderness (Isa. 35:1-10), which is then aligned with a
series of contemporary "wilderness" images: the South
Bronx, Vietnam, "assassins' bullets which kill the captains
and kings." The first of the short sermons ends with the
wilderness image explored "in the heart of those near you." A
T. S. Eliot quotation—"You neglect and belittle the desert. . . . The desert is squeezed in the tube-train with
you"—provides a visual context for this most immediate
expression of wilderness. There is a progression of images,
each one theologically congruent with the dominant biblical
image. Yet as each consequent image is developed, the
originating desert image gains more immediacy and power.
Within this model of the relationship of narrative and image,
the latter are overlaid like transparencies on an overhead
projector. The challenge here, though, is both to retain the
force and primacy of the biblical image while aligning it in
consciousness with readily available contemporary images.
Narrative is present at two levels in these Vannorsdall
sermons. The biblical story which gives birth to the
wilderness image is always in the background, though never
elaborated as a narrative system. Also implicitly present are
the contemporary stories which give rise to the desert images
of our experience. Although the sermon itself deals only in
the interplay of congruent biblical and contemporary images,
the intention of the method is that the implicit stories also
interlock within the theological context of the dominant
image and story of Israel's experience in the wilderness.

An alternative expression of the relationship between
narrative and image is modeled in Deneise Deter-Rankin's
sermon, "Just Look At Us Now" (pp. 186-89). This second
approach presumes a narrative scriptural plot as its structural
control (in this case, the parable of the prodigal son). The
introduction establishes that narrative line, but leaves off
with the younger son in the far country. What follows are two
modestly elaborated contemporary images that are locked

back into the parable both through theme and through the rhetorical device of a repetitive tag line ("Gimme. Give me."). Two more story-images expand on the experience of the son in the far country, though they are provided without explicit reference to the textual narrative. After a brief focus on the prodigal's decision to return, an image-laden contemporary story of return is developed followed by a wedding image which then comments on the older brother's resentment. Finally, the terse story of the seminarian reflects back to the returned prodigal, and the sermon concludes with a recapitulation of the images and a return to the conclusion of the parable.

This sermon represents an interesting and informative approach to preaching biblical narrative through its deft placement of contemporary images along the plot line of the pericope while leaving the biblical narrative itself mostly unspoken. Yet the logic and theological field of the parable remain intact and the sermon moves through the biblical story without becoming sidetracked. Obviously the appropriateness of the contemporary images to their place in the plot of the parable is decisive here, as is a necessary restraint in their development. Too much more narrative form at any point would make it difficult, if not impossible, for the hearers to continue their movement within the parabolic plot. And while the degree of explicitness of the story of the prodigal son could vary, Deter-Rankin aptly demonstrates a sermon which links the structure and movement of a biblical narrative with a series of contemporary images at points of significance. Through the use of her images, the hearers are invited into the world of the parable in a way that is both indirect and subtle, yet highly effective.

Beyond the two approaches to the interplay of narrative and image represented by the sermons of Vannorsdall and Deter-Rankin, other homiletical expressions of this relationship may be forthcoming. That two quite distinct models of preaching which embody a hermeneutic involving both narrative and image have been identified, however, is already significant and evocative. These approaches are significant since their implicit method calls the narrative homileticians to a deeper engagement along the lines previously suggested. What is evocative here is the promise that yet another path to a new hearing of the gospel may be available for biblical preaching. This implicit homiletic is less explored for now, but may become as fruitful for proclamation as the more well-traveled routes we have already surveyed.

THE WILDERNESS AND THE DRY LAND

John Vannorsdall

ISAIAH 35:1-10 (RSV)

"The wilderness and the dry land shall be glad,
the desert shall rejoice and blossom. . . ."

"You neglect and belittle the desert," wrote T. S. Eliot.
"The desert is not remote in southern tropics,
The desert is not only around the corner,
The desert is squeezed in the tube-train next to you,
The desert is in the heart of your brother."[34]

The desert is in the heart.

Faces parched and tongues thick, silently without strength we trudge in soft sand and see strange things which are not there. And when the wind blows, the sand moves, uncovering remnants of towns no longer living, and bony hand still clutching its sword, a soldier fallen in some long-finished battle. The desert is in the heart.

And when night comes, the cold lays claim, and we gather camel chips to make a little fire to keep away the immensity of cold and dark.

The wilderness and the dry land; they lie within the human heart.

Bethlehem lies just beyond the desert, and there is no other way, I think, of getting there than through the desert, if our journey is toward Bethlehem. At least God provided no other way for the Jews when they left Egypt on their journey, than forty years of desert. Whatever comfort of self-pity and self-righteousness may belong to a captive people was left behind. Now they faced themselves for a long time alone with God. They were a complaining rabble, it turned out, who'd rather bow before a golden calf they'd made than face the God who made them, rather eat leeks in Egypt than God's manna in the wilderness. They discovered that they were as much drawn to going back as they were to going forward, more drawn to what they already knew than by a promise and by what they could imagine of their future.

What the Jews could not stand was the journey, the wilderness and the dry land. The sand not good for dancing. The wind, when it came, moving the mounds to lay bare the bones of towns and soldiers. Fires too small at night to drive away the cold and dark.

The desert is in the American heart. Faces seared with the heat of South Bronx burning. Tongues which once sang of national glory parched and thickened with the fire of Vietnam. Assassins' bullets the desert scorpions which kill the captains and the kings. Sometimes the wind blows, the dunes move, and the remnants of a nation are seen, a great city, destiny manifest, a land of machines which danced and whirled. And the desert night is cold, the oil is nearly gone, and we gathered wood chips and a little coal for fire against the dark. The desert is in the American heart.

The desert is in the heart of those near you. In lives too little watered by tears of joy, too seldom refreshed by love letters, affirmations, friendly words, or healing touch by eye or hand. Seared and dry from constantly hacking it, too long trudging in the sand, too little dancing.

And Bethlehem lies just beyond the desert, and there is no other way, I think, of getting there than through the desert. And no one likes it here, alone with God, learning who and what we are, what craving we have for the leeks of Egypt, for remembered former security. As much drawn to going back as we are to going forward, and more drawn to what we knew than to what is promised.

"You neglect and belittle the desert," wrote T. S. Eliot. "The desert is squeezed in the tube-train with you." The desert is in the heart, so there's no journey toward Christmas which does not traverse the desert. I wonder when we'll get to Bethlehem? It's strange that the prophet who is supposed to guide says so little about where it is, and when we'll arrive. He says only that,

"The wilderness and the dry land shall be glad,
The desert shall rejoice and blossom."

JUST LOOK AT US NOW

Deneise Deter-Rankin

LUKE 15:11-32 (RSV)

"Father," he said in a voice too loud. "Father," said the son in a voice so brash it surprised even himself, "give me the share of property that falls to me." He did not ask for an advance on his allowance. The son did not even ask his father what he would think about handing over the inheritance a bit early. But—"Gimme. Hand it over. I'm sick of the slave-labor on this dust farm. There's a whole world out there and I want *my* piece of the pie! See ya." And "the younger son gathered all he had and took his journey into a far country, and there he squandered his property in loose living."

You know the grand piano in your mother's living room? The one that belonged to her mother? The one that was exhibited at the 1896 World's Fair? Didn't she tell you she'd leave it to you? Never did say what its appraised value was. But you have been asking around. In your new house you have this wonderful empty space right in front of the bay window looking down into the valley. Wouldn't it be perfect? If only. . . . "Father give me the share of property that falls to me." Gimme. Give me.

The stone arch over the entrance-way looks gothic in the approaching headlights. The dormitory looms in the dusk at the far end of campus. The trip has taken longer than you had remembered. The building is ablaze with light. When you cut the engine you realize all that noise is coming from one building. You and your daughter have carried a footlocker, six boxes of books, and a sweater chest up three flights of stairs. You open the stairwell door to step into the hall and there is no place to put your foot. The hall is wall-to-wall people. There is smoke. There is noise. Your daughter's room is at the other end of the hall. Footlocker in tow, you thread your way to number 360. Her roommate hands you a beer. Your daughter kisses you quick on the cheek. "Bye, Dad. See you Thanksgiving." She nudges you down the hall and down the first flight of stairs. "Drive safely. Oh. Hey, Dad. I need some money!" Gimme. Give me.

You took the training wheels off. You didn't want to take them off, but you did. You bit your lip. He wasn't ready. You knew he wasn't ready. You could have told him that. He didn't have his balance yet. And balance was the key. He begged you. So you took them off and covered your eyes. From the kitchen window you watched. He was starting off headed down-hill. That meant he wouldn't have to pedal, true. But what about brakes? He wobbled. A lot. And before the hill picked up too much momentum he tipped over and landed in the ditch. You bit your lip and you refrained from running outside to the rescue. From the kitchen window you could see he was O.K. At bedtime you bathed the wounded knee. And said not a word.

You know what it's like. Standing too close to the edge. The board hangs so far out that you can't see anything but water. Like looking down out of an airplane over the ocean. Nothing under you or beside you. Except water. Nothing to catch you. Nothing to fall back on. Your toes curl over the edge. You fight for balance. Going off the diving board for the first time. Who will catch you? Who will rescue you? Who will fish you out of the water? You are perched on the edge of the diving board. You know what it's like. To be that scared.

But it passes, doesn't it? When you paddle to the surface of the pool. When you are pulled out of the water by the armpits and wrapped in a sun-warm towel. Remember how weak your knees are for a while. And how your heart pounds. Lucky for you you have someone to turn to. Someone to take care of you. To fish you out of the pool. Someone you can just think about now to know they're there when you need—just to think about them. Who is it for you?

"And he arose and came to his father. But while he was yet at a distance, his father saw him and had compassion, and ran and embraced him and kissed him." How long have you picked your wounds over a family disagreement. Be honest. What's the record? Days, months, years? "And he arose and came to his father." What makes you "arise and come?" "And he had compassion on him, and ran and embraced him and kissed him." What makes you run? If you were right or if you were wrong? What makes you come home? What makes you open your arms to those who have decided to return?

You haven't been to see your parents for almost a year. Distance makes it hard. You have your own life now. It's not easy to get away. The longer you wait, the harder it becomes to go at all. Sometimes you are homesick. Even at your age. You imagine what it would be like. All those good smells. Big meals three times a day someone else has cooked for you. Someone gives you a stool for your feet. Someone turns on an extra light over your book so your eyes won't go bad. The nostalgia is almost enough to pack you off on that long drive winding down into the valley. Suddenly you remember what it was like the last time you were there: all that you wanted to accomplish; all you decided you had to prove before you would ever go home again.

You turn carefully down the hill into the driveway. That pothole has never been fixed. Headlights sweep across the front of the house. Windows are dark. It's late. You turn off the lights and roll silently down to the garage door. An old trick. You never should have come. It's not too late to drive back. Maybe they are asleep. Your eyes have adjusted to the dark. Your father is waiting on the front porch in his bathrobe. Something makes you open the car door. And the porch light goes on. Your mother's hair is not in curlers. They have been waiting up for you. Something makes you hurry into their arms.

Your sister's wedding was bigger than yours. She had more people. More presents. She had a train on her gown and a veil that followed her down the chapel steps long after she had reached the bottom. They went all-out. A sit-down dinner for hundreds. Flowers everywhere. And too much champagne. She was a beautiful bride with a row of attendants and so many friends. The party lasted for weeks. At the reception there was a big ugly fish on the buffet table with its head and eyes still there. Never had you seen such a show. Hers was what every girl dreams of when she's growing up. Yours was what you had when you got all grown and practical. But it makes you wonder. Hadn't your parents wanted all that pageantry and show for you too? They never said if they did. Maybe they weren't as proud of you and the man you married. You had good grades. You had been a pretty good kid. Did your parents like your sister better than you? Actually, *she* had been the partier. You had been kind of mild by comparison. And she had all those friends. All those parties. People who said she was the most beautiful bride. . . .

"Now his elder son was in the field; and as he came and drew near to the house, he heard music and dancing. . . . His father came out and entreated him, but he answered his father, 'Lo these many years I have served you and have never disobeyed your command; yet you never gave me a kid that I might make merry with my friends. But when this son of yours came, who has devoured your living with harlots, you killed for him the fatted calf!" And look at him now. Just look at him.

The seminary accepted him. The seminary gave him a fellowship. His home town was amazed. The church gave a reception the Sunday before he left. All his friends were there. They watched him from the punch bowl. "Remember the night his parents were out of town . . . after he wrecked his father's company car we thought . . . his fraternity was cra-zy . . . it's a wonder he survived . . . when he dove into the shallow end no one thought . . . said it was a miracle . . . and to look at him now." Just look at him now.

And look at us. Standing on the porch of a darkened house in our slippers watching for our daughter or son to return safely home. Coveting a family piano. Demanding that the training wheels come off. Standing on the edge of the diving board. Worried that our brothers and sisters have been dealt a better hand than we. Uncertain. And afraid. Greedy. Alone. Trying to remember who it is we turn to when there is nowhere else to turn. Just look at us now. "Father, give me the share of property that falls to me. . . . Father, I have sinned against heaven and before you; I am no longer worthy to be called your son." Just look at us now. "Bring quickly the best robe, and put it on him; and put a ring on his hand, and shoes on his feet; and bring the fatted calf and kill it, and let us eat and make merry; for this my son was dead, and is alive again; he was lost, and is found." And look at us now. Just look!

NOTES

1. Stephen Crites, "The Narrative Quality of Experience," *Journal of the American Academy of Religion* 39, no. 3 (September 1971), pp. 291-311. With reference to the literary-critical and philosophical investigations into the nature of narrative see, for example, Robert Scholes and Robert Kellogg, *The Nature of Narrative* (London: Oxford University Press, 1966) and Paul Ricoeur, *Essays on Biblical Interpretation,* ed. Lewis S. Mudge (Philadelphia: Fortress Press, 1980).

2. See, for example, Terrence W. Tilley, *Story Theology* (Wilmington, Delaware: Michael Glazier, 1985) and Sallie McFague, *Metaphorical Theology: Models of God in Religious Language* (Philadelphia: Fortress Press, 1982).

3. Michael Goldberg, *Theology and Narrative: A Critical Introduction* (Nashville: Abingdon Press, 1981). See chapter VI, "The Story of our Life," for an excellent survey of the recent development of narrative hermeneutics and theology.

4. James McClendon, Jr., *Biography as Theology* (Nashville: Abingdon Press, 1974), p. 96; Stanley Hauerwas, *The Peaceable Kingdom: A Primer in Christian Ethics* (Notre Dame, Ind.: University of Notre Dame Press, 1983); Stanley Hauerwas, *A Community of Character* (Notre Dame: University of Notre Dame Press, 1980); Jerome Berryman, "Being in Parables with Children," *Religious Education* 74, no. 3 (May-June 1979), pp. 271-85; John H. Westerhoff III, *A Pilgrim People: Learning Through the Church Year* (Minneapolis, Minn.: Seabury Press, 1984).

5. Cf. Robert Alter, *The Art of Biblical Narrative* (New York: Basic Books, 1981).

6. Readers are referred to the "Selected Bibliography" collected by Pheme Perkins in *Hearing the Parables of Jesus* (New York: Paulist Press, 1981), pp. 212-16. Also, note Bernard Brandon Scott, *Jesus, Symbol-Maker for the Kingdom* (Philadelphia: Fortress Press, 1981).

7. Goldberg, *Theology and Narrative,* p. 244.

8. Ibid., p. 213.

9. Hauerwas, *The Peaceable Kingdom,* p. 29.

10. Ibid., p. 28.

11. Ibid., p. 29.

12. Ibid.

13. Austin Farrer, *The Glass of Vision* (Westminster, England: Dacre Press, 1948).

14. McClendon, *Biography as Theology,* p. 96.

15. Ibid., p. 99.

16. Donald L. Weismann, *Language and Visual Form* (Austin: Univ. of Texas Press, 1968), p. 41.

17. Wesley Kort, *Narrative Elements and Religious Meaning* (Philadelphia: Fortress Press, 1975), p. 67.

18. Austin Farrer refers to these primal images with Spinoza's term, *experientia vaga,* "loose experience." Farrer, *Glass of Vision,* p. 26.

19. David Harned notes that because of their concreteness, "images are more important for the exercise of human agency than are conceptual prescriptions." David Harned, *Images for Self-Recognition: The Christian as Player, Sufferer and Vandal* (New York: Seabury Press, 1977), p. 2.

20. Ibid., p. 133.
21. Ibid. Images then can be renamed as they experience dislocation from one story and relocation in another.
22. Weismann, *Language and Visual Form*, p. 42.
23. Ibid., p. 44.
24. Harned, *Images for Self-Recognition*, p. 134.
25. Ibid.
26. Ibid., p. 155.
27. Alla Bozarth-Campbell, *The Word's Body: An Incarnational Aesthetic of Interpretation* (University, Ala.: University of Alabama Press, 1979), p. 104.
28. See Leonide Ouspensky, *Theology of the Icon* (Crestwood, N.Y.: St. Vladimir's Seminary Press, 1978), pp. 39 ff. To speak of "iconic imagery" is technically redundant, but perhaps necessary given the conventional meanings usually assigned to the term "image."
29. See Gordon W. Lathrop, "A Rebirth of Images: On the Use of the Bible in Liturgy," *Worship* 58, no. 4 (July 1984): pp. 291-304.
30. Bozarth-Campbell, *The Word's Body*, p. 107.
31. John W. Vannorsdall, *Dimly Burning Wicks* (Philadelphia: Fortress Press, 1982).
32. John Vannorsdall, "Esthetics and Preaching," *dialog* 20, no. 2 (Spring 1981), p. 102.
33. Ibid., pp. 102-4.
34. T. S. Eliot, "Choruses from 'The Rock'," in *Collected Poems, 1909-1962* (N.Y.: Harcourt Brace Jovanovich, 1930), p. 149.